OVERCOMING AGORAPHOBIA

Muriel Frampton

Many thousands of people in the world today are imprisoned in their homes by fear. They are ordinary, intelligent men and women, who used to lead normal lives until, suddenly, they became afraid to go out.

They cannot explain the fear. Their friends are completely baffled by it. Family life is affected. They ask the question 'Why does it happen?', but can find no answer, and this makes it more frightening. Victims are often told that the cause is unimportant.

The author of this book—a psychotherapist—does not agree. She explains the emotional background which lies behind the phobia, and goes on to demonstrate how, when the *true* cause is known, not only is relief and cure possible, but the deeper needs of the patient can be met as never before. *Wholeness* of personality is the end result.

This book shows how agoraphobia can be cured. For those who are unable to get to a therapist for treatment, suggestions are given for self-help, both by analytic methods and through desensitization techniques.

With warm understanding and concern, the author points the way forward to freedom and fulfillment, and encourages the patient to take the first step.

OVERCOMING AGORAPHOBIA

OVERCOMING AGORAPHOBIA
Coping with the World Outside

by

MURIEL FRAMPTON
B.D., B.Com.

St. Martin's Press   New York

CONTENTS

FOREWORD

No more important discovery for the welfare of mankind has emerged in this century than psychoanalysis. But so far only a tiny fraction of the population has come within reach of its benefits. It is relatively unrecognized. By far the great majority of our overworked psychiatrists in the National Health Service, though appreciative of Freud's work, are not trained in psychoanalysis, and at present there exists a wide gap between this highly expensive yet invaluable treatment, and the numberless thousands of ordinary men and women who desperately need it.

As far as agoraphobia is concerned, it is this gap that this present volume seeks to span. Written in homely sympathetic style, it opens the ordinary sufferer's eyes to the true causes of his crushing malady, encourages deep insight, and so makes possible relief and even cure.

In contrast to the orthodox psychiatric approach to the problem of agoraphobia, Muriel Frampton embarks on an effort to explain in easy everyday language the deep unconscious motivations that produce this widespread illness. Alas, too many psychiatrists — because of lack of time or training — treat the symptoms of this handicap either by drugs or by a series of 'behaviourist' contrivances, designed to jockey the sufferer into a situation where he — or she — forgets to be afraid. These manipulations of personality may help some sufferers and bring elements of relief, but they do not lay the foundations of a more adequate personality liberated from further flights into agoraphobia.

The author of this book rightly emphasizes that she is not seeking to eliminate this or that *symptom*, still less to encourage the patient to tolerate or 'live with it' but, by understanding on a deep level, to make possible the growth of a more adequate self with which to face life and its challenges.

If you are a victim of phobias, do not treat this book as a magic wand for instant relief. This book conceals as well as reveals valuable analytic insights. Only as you read it over and over again, mark passages in it that 'ring bells' in your mind, and work consistently on its suggestions, will you come to enjoy the release it offers.

One word about the author. Handicapped in infancy by poliomyelitis which left her with a permanent limp, she faced life bravely and soon gave evidence of marked versatility. Apart from graduating in the contrasting fields of economics and divinity she also became an Associate of Trinity College, London, and a Licentiate of the Royal Academy of Music. For years she lectured in economics and accountancy, then, still unsatisfied, she subjected herself to a rigorous psycho-analytic training for her present vocation as a psycho-therapist, because in so doing, she felt she could best help suffering people. The quality of her understanding and dedication shines out in this book as it does in her psychotherapeutic practice. I commend the book heartily.

C. EDWARD BARKER

INTRODUCTION

Agoraphobia afflicts thousands of people in many different countries. In the industrialized nations especially, with their huge urban complexes, their sky-scraper blocks and constant rush and roar of heavy traffic, there are those who have become afraid to leave their homes lest they be overcome by fear. Only those who suffer from agoraphobia, or live with someone afflicted with this fear, know the misery involved.

A person who has lived a successful life, shouldered responsibilities, and travelled about quite freely may suddenly, for no obvious reason, become a victim of fear. He, or she, begins to tremble like a leaf at the prospect of having to make a short journey and may not even be able to get as far as the sidewalk without being overwhelmed by panic. It all seems so inexplicable.

The distress of the agoraphobic person is aggravated by the knowledge that the rest of the family are suffering as well. The mother who cannot see her daughter receive an honor at the school awards ceremony, or watch her son captain the college sports team, blames herself for her children's disappointment.

The holiday season is a nightmare. Other youngster go on outings and away for holidays with their parents. The mother who is a victim of agoraphobia is all too well aware of this norm, and for the sake of the children she may try to be brave and promise to take part in holiday activities. But just at the last minute she may be utterly defeated and in a flood of tears.

If her husband is in a position that demands some sharing of social life she feels that, by her inability to accompany him, she is letting him down and involving him in awkward explanations.

No one in the family seems to understand, which is not surprising: the afflicted member does not know what has happened either. It is all so bewildering, and apparently hopeless.

How can you put something right, when you do not really know what is wrong?

It is the purpose of this book to help those who suffer in this way, and to help their families, by:

1. explaining the 'inexplicable' – pointing to possible, and indeed probable, causes of the trouble.
2. describing the forms of professional help available.
3. making suggestions for self-help.

In regard to the last point, I particularly bear in mind the fact that, for obvious reasons, the agoraphobic cannot easily travel to a professional psychotherapist or hospital for treatment. It may therefore be necessary for him to practise self-help, at least in the early stages.

It is *not* my purpose here to give suggestions for 'living with' agoraphobia, that is, making life more tolerable and interesting within the context of the restrictions suffered. As a therapist, it is my primary aim to work for *healing*. This does not mean that I am unaware of the need for interim help with practical problems. These vary so much from one agoraphobic to another, however, that I feel the particular needs of individuals can best be met by personal contact of some kind.

In several countries self-help clubs have been set up which provide such contact for phobic patients. In the United Kingdom, for instance, The Open Door was started some eight years ago by a former agoraphobic sufferer, and many thousands of people have joined since its inception.

Such an organization can do a lot to assist victims of the phobia by giving practical help, guidance and encouragement based on an understanding of the problem.

There is a danger, of course, that a patient might use the club merely as a prop to support him in his trouble, rather than as a means of finding release. Odd though it sounds, even the feeling of 'belonging' sometimes acts as a resistance to recovery. (I explain this factor of resistance in Chapter X.)

The Open Door has no counterpart in the United States, but in California there is a nonprofit organization which operates nationwide to help agoraphobics. It is called Terrap (standing for 'territorial apprehensiveness').

Unlike The Open Door, Terrap operates under the direction of a psychiatrist (Dr A. B. Hardy) and exist primarily to offer courses of instruction for recovery, rather than merely to put phobics in touch with each other to discuss problems. At one time a 'buddy' system was tried out by Terrap, but it was discarded when Terrap found that the phobics in this program tended to pick up each other's phobias, thus adding to their own difficulties.

Terrap offers various self-help programs as well as group therapy sessions for those able to attend. For those at a distance, help and advice can be given by telephone and a quarterly newsletter is sent to subscribers.

Though personal therapy is available to a limited extent, the emphasis is on group therapy, and of course not everyone suffering from agoraphobia is enthusiastic about this approach. In many cases the motivation needed to get to the meetings will be insufficient.

Moreover, the programs aim at rehabilitation, rather than regrowth and healing of the personality. This can only come through analytic insight.

Many testify to the help they have received from Terrap, however, and if you would like further details of its activities and scale of charges, write to Terrap, 1010 Doyle Street, Menlo Park, California 94025.

In any case I would advise readers to make the fullest use of facilities available at local clinics, most of which are affiliated with hospitals. Your local doctor should be able to give you the necessary information and referral.

But whatever form of help you seek, for yourself or another, always remember that without the phobic person's own motivation towards recovery, nothing will be achieved.

One final word of explanation about the book: it treats the problem of agoraphobia, and its cure, purely from the psychological point of view. There may be those who will wonder why, as a person with religious faith, I have not offered that as the way, *par excellence*, of overcoming fear.

Experience has taught me, however, that where there is *repressed* fear, conflict, guilt or insecurity, the person's religious outlook is itself coloured by unconscious emotional dis-ease.

This is not to suggest that religious faith is of no help. Far from it. I have often brought my faith to bear on my own conscious fears, with very positive results. But it is all too easy to give a pat answer along religious lines, without appreciating that the sufferer probably knows this answer already, but is unable to assimilate it fully into his unconscious emotional life.

It seems preferable, therefore, to confine myself to a strictly psychological approach, rather than give inadequate and oversimplified religious answers which might unintentionally give rise to increased conflict and suffering.

This is, then, a book of practical psychology, intended to give insight and encouragement to phobic sufferers. The book was first published in the United Kingdom by Thorsons Publishers Limited (at whose suggestion it was written), and it is the author's sincere wish that its publication in the United States will bring help and release to many more victims of this most distressing phobia.

PART I
UNDERSTANDING

CHAPTER ONE

WHAT IS AGORAPHOBIA?

A 'phobia' is a fear which a person knows to be irrational and exaggerated, but which he simply cannot control. For example, a man who is otherwise quite tough may turn green at the thought of going up in an aeroplane. You may tell him that far more people are killed on the roads than in air crashes. It will make no difference. He cannot reason himself out of the fear.

I am sure you already know of several different phobias. Many women have an exaggerated fear of mice and spiders. Perhaps you know someone who has a fear of heights (acrophobia); and most people have heard of claustrophobia – the fear of enclosed spaces.

Yet the term 'agoraphobia' was almost unknown until fairly recent years. People who were afraid to venture out from their homes were just thought of as peculiar. At first, perhaps, they received sympathy, but as their condition persisted or worsened their families became irritated and critical, or tried with kind intentions to laugh (or bully) them out of it. Their trouble was neither understood, nor recognized for what it was. Nor was it realized just how many suffer from this affliction.

The Term 'Agoraphobia'
The word 'agoraphobia' is derived from two Greek words – 'phobos' meaning 'fear', and 'agora' meaning 'a place of assembly, or market-place'. It is, then, the 'fear of public places'. The victims of the phobia describe it in different ways, according to their own symptoms. One will say it is the

'fear of open spaces' while another says it is a 'fear of crowds', or a 'fear of leaving home'.

Agoraphobes (as such patients are called) are by no means rare, so if you are a victim of this fear you must not think you are alone and peculiar in your predicament. There are all too many people who suffer from this phobia: it is estimated, in fact, that there are about a quarter of a million agoraphobes in the country today.

People Affected in Different Ways

Patients vary enormously in the degree to which their lives are handicapped by the phobia. One patient, for example, is able to go out fairly happily provided she is in the company of someone else.

Another woman is unable to leave the house at all. As soon as she gets outside the garden gate she feels dizzy and faint. Her legs seem just like jelly, and she retreats in panic to her front door and shuts herself in once more.

A young mother has told how for a time she really felt safe only *in bed*, and in fact spent the major part of her days in the bedroom.

Recently one man spoke to me of his wife's dilemma. 'She appears to be a perfectly normal person', he said. 'You'd never think there was anything wrong with her. But she cannot walk across a street alone. Yet she can *drive* anywhere. In fact, she is a marvellous driver. I just cannot understand it.'

A young man came to me for help with the opposite problem: he goes out and about fairly freely, but feels quite unsafe when driving his car, especially on a broad, straight road like a motorway.

The problem of one young wife, severely agoraphobic, centres around her fear of being seen. She is willing to go into the garden to play with the children, but on no account will she have her photograph taken with them — not even if she herself is in the house, looking at them through a window.

There are countless different ways in which individuals are affected. The *width* of the street is often significant. One patient may be terrified of venturing into a wide street, while another is equally fearful of a narrow one. A sudden *change* of width is nearly always upsetting.

In some cases the phobia gets such a hold that it becomes not only a fear of going out, but a dread of being alone, even in the house. The whole of life, in fact, becomes fraught with fear and panic. There is a desperate need to make contact, and life becomes almost impossible without the daily phone call to one's mother or daughter, or a friend.

The Need For a Way of Escape
The agoraphobe fears especially those situations in which he feels he has no way of escape. For this reason if he *does* go to a theatre or cinema he makes sure he can get a gangway seat. At any social gatherings he will find a seat near the door.

Only with the greatest reluctance will such a patient board a bus, and if he does, he will likewise sit or stand near the door. An injunction to 'move down the bus, please' will cause him to tremble like a leaf, and he may well murmur some excuse to get off the bus before he has reached his destination, rather than suffer the agonies of the situation.

One patient could drive his own car quite cheerfully, but whenever he was a passenger in any vehicle driven by another person he would break out in a sweat, because he was not free to stop the vehicle when he wanted. He felt trapped.

Similarly, journeys abroad are definitely out, for one cannot get off a ship or plane just when a fit of panic strikes!

It can be seen that life becomes very restricted indeed when once the phobia gets a hold, and not infrequently the patient ends up by not going out of the house at all.

The Prevalence of the Phobia
One of the reasons why agoraphobia is so prevalent (it is estimated that two or three people in every thousand of the population suffer from it) is that almost any phobia may be quickly translated into a fear of going out. If you are afraid of cats, for example, you dread going out in case you see one. If you have a phobia about receiving infection, you will soon

reach the point of staying indoors. It has been estimated that sixty per cent of all phobics suffer from agoraphobia as one of their symptoms.

Unfortunately, when once the fear of going out has established itself, its hold on the sufferer tends to become more and more firm. Why is this? One of the reasons is that staying in the house is a habit that is formed very easily, almost unconsciously, and may get a hold before one realizes it.

The Phobia of Every Day

In the case of some phobias, the situation can be avoided for the most part, or it arises only occasionally. For instance, it is not every day that one sees a mouse, or experiences a thunderstorm. A person who is afraid of heights can generally avoid the situations in which he would find himself in a panic. The man who is terrified of flying may be able to use other means of transport.

The agoraphobic patient, on the other hand, is *continually* made aware of his difficulty. He has to contend with his phobia every single day – and if he gives into it, it very soon becomes firmly entrenched.

It Has To Be Faced in Public

Moreover, whereas one can attempt to overcome some types of fear in the privacy of one's own home, or in the company of friends, in the nature of the case agoraphobia can only be overcome by venturing in public, and facing the possibility of a panic in public. Now this is a very different matter, because it is, in fact, the very core of the fear.

Indeed one writer has suggested that agoraphobia is wrongly named. It is not, he says, 'fear of public places' but the 'fear of being afraid'. By this he means that agoraphobes are not afraid of the street, or the bus or train, as such. Rather, they are afraid of being overwhelmed by fear in such places, where they are unable to find supportive help. It is the *panic* in a public place which they dread.

In this way the phobia is perpetuated. For it is one thing

to make a brave attempt to overcome a fear in private: it is quite another to risk embarrassment in a public place.

Women More Than Men

Any person may become the victim of a phobia, but it is interesting to find that ninety per cent of phobic patients are women. Certainly it is true that agoraphobia, in particular, is much more common among women than men. You may wonder why this is, and I would suggest several contributory factors.

In the first place, a man normally has little choice but to go out and earn a living. There are few jobs which he is likely to do at home. This means that the habit does not so easily get a chance to become established. Despite the anxiety he suffers, he is forced to make the effort.

Moreover, his weakness is readily apparent if he remains at home and leaves his wife to go out to earn a living for both of them. He would be embarrassed by such an arrangement, so he has a strong incentive to face his fear, and put up with the difficulty he experiences.

A woman on the other hand is usually in a different situation. Indeed she can actually fulfil herself in the home to a much greater extent than is possible for her husband. A man tied to the house will probably get so bored that he will make every effort to go out! In doing this he is also helping himself, for as he faces his fear it will lessen rather than increase. I shall have more to say on that in a later chapter.

Secondly – despite the Women's Lib. movement – the social climate probably still tends to boost the male ego rather than the female. Many parents, for example, are especially pleased when they are blessed with a boy, and this is particularly true of the mother, on whom a baby is more dependent for acceptance at the very beginning of life. It is no mere coincidence that ego-weakness, one of the contributory factors in agoraphobia, is found more generally in women than in men.

Thirdly, it is also probably true that frustration of sexual desire is more common among women than among men. The reasons for this lie partly in their differing attitudes to sex and promiscuity, partly in the imbalance of sex distribution in certain age groups, and in many other factors. Agoraphobia which stems from a deep-rooted sexual conflict (as it does in *some* cases) is therefore more likely to affect women.

On the Increase

It does seem that agoraphobia is more prevalent today than it used to be. One must remember, of course, that only in recent years, since the phobia has been recognized and treated, have many people come forward for help. In the past there have been many cases (and indeed there still are) which are quite unknown to the people who compile statistics. Such folk have retired into their homes and confided their problems to very few people; their distress remains a private matter and there is no record of their illness.

It is well-known, however, that symptoms of nervous strain and tension *are* more prevalent today than ever before, and no doubt the incidence of agoraphobia reflects this general trend.

CHAPTER TWO

THE SYMPTOMS OF AGORAPHOBIA

The physical effects vary from person to person, but certain symptoms are commonly experienced during an 'attack'. Giddiness often occurs, for example, with palpitations or difficulty in breathing. Unfortunately, if you suffer like this you may fear that there is something physically wrong with you, and this increases the panic. You become even *more* reluctant to go far from home in case you have an attack.

In actual fact you are probably perfectly healthy. In any case it is better to have a check-up with your doctor, than refuse to go out for fear that you may have a heart attack. When you know you are in good health, you can tackle the *real* reasons for your fear, which are emotional.

Another common symptom is the feeling that one's legs just will not function. Either they feel wobbly (jelly-legs is quite an apt description), or they feel as heavy as lead, with no freedom of movement in them. Again it is important to realize that this 'weakness' is only a natural result of tension and stress. It is not an indication of some physical defect.

The same thing applies to many other symptoms felt by agoraphobes and nervous sufferers generally. Choking feelings, sweating, headaches, 'churning' of the stomach — these are quite usual accompaniments of tension, though I will not embark here on an explanation of the biological reasons for them.

If you suffer in this way, it may help if you remember that every one of us has known something of these symptoms in times of stress.

The nervous speaker, for instance, finds his mouth becomes so dry just before he is called on to deliver his address, that he rapidly takes a glass of water if it is available. Even so he may wonder whether he can manage to get the words out.

The music student is dismayed when her hands start to tremble and perspire as she waits her turn to play before the examiners.

Which of us has not experienced 'butterflies' in the stomach when we have attended some important interview or performed at some public function?

Such symptoms are a *perfectly normal* outcome of tension, and generally we manage to put up with them because we know that they are only temporary and will disappear as soon as the cause of the stress is past.

Unfortunately, to the victim of agoraphobia these physical discomforts cause not merely temporary embarrassment but panic and hysterical anxiety and, not infrequently, a flood of tears.

Overwhelmed

Apart from the physical symptoms of stress, many agoraphobes suffer from an awful dread of being overwhelmed, and feelings of unreality which can be very frightening.

A young student told me how, after returning to college after one vacation, she went through this experience. If she went into a crowded store, or even into a busy street she felt quite overwhelmed by the crowds and the traffic. She did not even want to be with her own group of friends. It was all too much for her. There was an awful feeling of unreality which terrified her, and she was thankful that a short course of relaxation treatment put her right again.

More General Characteristics

Indecision is something which plagues *many* nervous sufferers — not to mention their families! This is particularly so in the case of the agoraphobic patient, who tends to be courageous and optimistic one day, and is then overcome by fear and despair the next. She may want to see a particular production at the local theatre, and be determined to make the effort. Her husband gets the tickets in advance, thinking it will encourage her, but at the very last minute she finds she cannot face it.

Holidays are an even greater problem, as bookings have to be made so long in advance and the payment of a deposit is often involved. There are the children to consider too. They are too young and full of spirits to understand their mother's difficulty. They feel let down, and this only piles on the agony for the mother who feels guilty and responsible for their disappointment.

Little Initiative
The agoraphobe who cannot make her own decisions often ends up by falling in with whatever other people suggest. She has no confidence in herself to take the initiative in anything, and appears apathetic and lacking in interest. Indeed, she *is* apathetic very often, for any kind of prolonged nervous stress is debilitating. So much energy goes into dealing with the emotional struggle that one's reserves are depleted. There is little joy or excitement in life. One's whole existence becomes a battle against fear, apathy, guilt and depression.

Again so much depends on the individual's own background and temperament. I know of one young mother who appears to accept her restricted life quite happily, as long as no one tries to bully her to go out. If she can be left alone to do as she likes she seems to be perfectly content. But if she thinks anyone is going to ask her to go anywhere, she 'stops them' even before they have asked.

This 'acceptance' is not, of course, something which I am commending to you. I want to help you to go forward to find freedom, rather than to accept your confinement to the house.

Aggressiveness
Many agoraphobic patients find themselves somewhat short-tempered and aggressive with the family, and with friends who try to help them.

The general complaint behind it all is: 'You just don't

understand'. As I have said before, this is indeed true. The phobia is quite bewildering to other people as well as to the patient and, what is more, the family is involved in the effects of it.

If you suffer an accident and find yourself in hospital, or if you become seriously ill, you may receive lots of sympathy, get-well cards and loving attention from the family.

But this is different. You are involving your family in your suffering, and because they can see no good reason for it, they resent it. Or they try to chivvy you out of it — which *you* resent.

Their lack of understanding is hard to bear, and serves to increase your difficulty. You feel guilty on the one hand, yet you feel hurt and badly used, even spiteful about it all. It is also true that the state of tension in which you so often find yourself makes you edgy and nervy — ready to fly off the handle quickly. So now you have a second source of guilt — your own aggression.

Strained Relationships

Unfortunately, as the agoraphobic patient becomes more and more withdrawn into his, or her, restricted life, relationships easily become strained. A couple who used to be very happy together may be driven apart, each blaming the other for a lack of understanding. The husband may come to feel that his wife is not prepared to *try* to overcome her trouble and share life with him as she used to do. The wife is so preoccupied with her daily fight against feelings of terror and panic that she can no longer be 'outward looking'. She becomes introspective and (understandably) concerned primarily for herself. Every morning she wakes up with only one thought in her mind: how to 'get through the day'. This constant struggle absorbs so much of her inner resources that she can raise little interest in the affairs of other people.

This is the situation at its worst, but happily things are not always as bad as that. Sometimes the sufferer is blessed with a very understanding partner, who is prepared to be patient and loving. In other cases the patient is not so withdrawn as this, and can enter imaginatively and sympathetically into the life of the other members of the family.

Intolerance

Patients who are severely agoraphobic often display another characteristic trait: an intolerance of other people's difficulties. It may seem strange that patients who so often complain of a lack of understanding of their own problems should be unsympathetic towards the sufferings of other people.

Yet it is true that agoraphobes regard other phobias as far less debilitating and agonizing than their own fearful state. There may be some justification for this, but it is also true that one has to experience the difficulties of another person to know what can be involved. Mrs Neville, of 'The Open Door', has reported receiving letters from some two hundred 'spider phobics' in one year, and she discovered that it could be almost as crippling as agoraphobia.

Even within the ranks of agoraphobes one finds patients who are 'jealous' about the use of the term 'agoraphobia'. Someone who is not *totally* unable to go out may be told he does not really suffer from agoraphobia at all!

It is also interesting to hear from 'The Open Door' that ex-agoraphobics can be very intolerant of those who are still victims of the phobia. This seems even more strange. Perhaps the people concerned have found their own recovery easier than they expected; it could be that their own problems were not so deeply rooted as those of other people.

So much depends upon the degree to which the phobia restricts the person. Some patients are caught up in a general state of chronic anxiety, of which agoraphobia is just one manifestation. They suffer exaggerated fears in almost any situation, not just in the matter of going out of the house. There are others who show scarcely any abnormality except in one particular regard – say, crossing a road alone.

Many patients suffer from claustrophobic tendencies in certain situations, and I shall deal with this in some detail in a later chapter.

So much for the symptoms of agoraphobia. They add up to a great deal of misery, for the patient most of all, but also for members of the family, whose social life becomes more difficult and restricted.

Is there a way out? Fortunately there is. In the following chapters we shall be looking at the causes of agoraphobia. When we know something of these we shall be in a better position to see the way forward to a cure.

CHAPTER THREE

PRECIPITATING CAUSES

It has been found that many patients suffering from agoraphobia can trace the beginning of their trouble to some embarrassing incident, or situation of severe stress, which affected them to such a calamitous extent that they became unduly terrified of the same thing happening again. We say that the incident caused them to be 'sensitized'.

One woman patient, for example, suddenly experienced a violent attack of vertigo (dizziness) at a London theatre. The experience was so devastating to her that she *dreaded* the possibility of it recurring. Afterwards, if ever she went to the theatre, she made sure beforehand that she could obtain a seat by the aisle. Before long she gave up going to places of entertainment altogether, and eventually could not face going out at all. She became a prisoner in her own home, held there by fear.

Another patient, whose case is related by Dr J.A. Hadfield,[1] experienced a severe panic one night in the desert during the war. He was going from his office to the officers' mess, as he had done regularly every evening at that same time. But on this occasion the darkness and the solitariness filled him with horror. He was sensitized by it, and for years afterwards he could not cross a park or even a street alone.

I know of another agoraphobic, a young wife, whose phobia dates back to a ride in the car with her family, when she suddenly clutched at her throat in a dreadful fit of panic

---

[1] Dr J.A. Hadfield: *Psychology and Mental Health*, Allen & Unwin.

and begged to be taken home at once. She has scarcely ever left the house since that day.

Traumatic Events

In some cases it is easy to understand the stress and tension which have sensitized the patient. In the case of a woman, for example, the shock of losing a baby at birth, or the emotional and physical strains of a difficult confinement, are very natural causes of severe stress. An unmarried mother may likewise be so caught up in feelings of guilt and the fear of condemnation that she is more easily sensitized, and becomes fearful of going out.

A state of acute shock following a major operation, or a sudden bereavement, may mobilize anxieties that have been latent over many years. Such traumatic events may leave the person wanting in self-confidence, fearful of meeting with other people, and lacking in interest in the world outside. This state of mind provides just the soil in which the seeds of agoraphobia can start to grow, for it tends to establish the habit of remaining at home instead of going out.

Trifling Incidents

Sometimes a really trivial incident will precipitate such a state of panic that it leaves the victim completely baffled. One woman's agoraphobia was triggered off by something which happened on holiday, while she was taking a walk with some friends in the late evening. Her foot slipped as she was going along the tow path by a river, and although she was in no actual danger of falling into the water, the incident left her completely unnerved, in a state of unbelievable panic. From then on she began to go out less and less, until she was unable to leave her home at all.

Another patient dated his fears of going out to an incident in the wartime black-out, when he bumped into a lamp post in the dark. He found his heart pounding at a terrible pace, or so it seemed to him, and he was shocked and terrified to an extent quite out of keeping with the nature of the occurrence.

Bewilderment Adds To the Fear

Such an experience is completely bewildering to the person concerned, and the very fact that it seems so inexplicable only serves to increase the anxiety.

If any of my readers have relatives or friends who suffer in this way I want you to understand the importance of what I have just stated. If a person knows *why* he has panicked he can face the issue involved, and is better able to help himself. He may even be able to avoid such situations in future as far as possible. But if he finds himself caught in such a devastating experience *without any apparent reason*, he is left with no knowledge of what caused it or when it could occur again. This uncertainty greatly increases his anxiety.

Such apparently trifling causes are, of course, more likely to sensitize a person if his nerves are already at a low ebb. But in any case, they betray the existence of much deeper fears, which have been mobilized by the incident. We shall look at these more closely in the next chapter.

Prolonged Stress

Sometimes a patient becomes sensitized, not by a sudden shock, but as a result of prolonged stress. A long and debilitating illness, for example, can be very wearing, physically and mentally and also emotionally. Negative attitudes take over.

If you have experienced this, you will know what I mean: the tendency to give in to the illness, to retreat from life, rather than take up your responsibilities again. Even the compensations of being ill – the sympathy, friendly visits, gifts of flowers etc. – may be a subtle encouragement to remain housebound in semi-invalidism rather than take up the threads of life once more.

Continued tension of any kind – from frustration, eco-nomic worries, harrassment, or just plain overwork (especially where it is not done for one's own satisfaction and pleasure, but in circumstances involving a feeling of injustice and hardship) – leaves the nervous system depleted and renders a person vulnerable: liable to become over-sensitive and caught up in an anxiety state. In such circumstances the least discomfort or extra demand, an unexpected shock, the slightest accident, can give rise to panic.

Obsessive Fear

If the panic is sufficiently great it becomes itself the object of a further fear, as some of you know only too well. 'What is happening to me?', you ask yourself. 'Is this a heart attack? Or am I going mental?' Almost certainly it is neither, but you are so perplexed and worried that you do not know what to think. The whole episode becomes fraught with embarrassment and terror and you are caught in a vicious circle. What started as a sudden experience of panic, or chronic nervous fatigue, now becomes an obsessive fear.

The Threat From Within

As I said in Chapter One, this is not so much the fear of certain external situations, but a *fear of being caught in a panic*, with no supportive help available.

It is this subjective element which distinguishes agoraphobia from many other phobias – the thing one fears is one's own reactions. The street, the bus or train, is not felt to be dangerous in itself. The danger is in oneself, or so it feels. As one patient remarked: 'I seem to be at the mercy of something inside myself over which I have no control, and which I do not understand.'

This is just it: a fear of uncontrollable panic in a place where no help is available and where there is no means of escape.

Why?

One question will, I know, be in your mind, which I have not yet dealt with. 'Why does it happen?' After all, most people can contain their anxieties; they experience panic only in proportion to the facts of the situation. *Why*, then, do some people react in an exaggerated way, and become permanently handicapped by fears that are quite unjustified?

To find the answer to that question we must look more

closely at the factors which influence our emotional development. We shall do that in the next chapter.

CHAPTER FOUR

GOING DEEPER

In this chapter I want to deal with the problem in the light of depth psychology – that is, from the analytic point of view.

So far, we have discussed the various ways in which a person may become sensitized to a fear of going out. It may be a sudden shock or traumatic experience, or a slow nervous exhaustion which leaves the emotional resources at a low ebb.

But *why* is it that one person becomes unduly sensitized by an emotional trauma which another person is able to ride successfully? To some extent, we are all liable to be thrown off balance emotionally on occasions, but most of us manage to recover our equilibrium in a short time. Why, then, are some unfortunate people overwhelmed, and increasingly held in the grip of fear?

I have said that a sudden shock, however slight, may mobilize fears that have been latent for many years. I want now to explain what I meant by this.

If you are suffering from agoraphobia yourself, you know only too well that your panic is out of all proportion to the situation. The rational part of you, your intellect, is quite aware of this. You have probably tried already to argue yourself out of your fear. You have condemned yourself for 'being so silly'. But it is to no avail. You cannot reason with this fear. It goes deeper than that.

The Right Context
Yes, your fear is illogical in your present-day circumstances. But there *is* a reason for it, and your panic can be understood

when it is seen *in its right context* — that is, in the light of an earlier emotional experience which was so devastating that it was heavily repressed. It has been 'forcefully forgotten' by the conscious mind, but the memory of it is stored away in the unconscious; it still forms part of your experience.

If anything should happen which has associations with that fear and insecurity of infancy, you experience once again the original feeling of panic — even though you cannot remember the early situation to which it relates. To put it in a more formal way: when the original experience is approximated, the original feelings are reproduced, whether the memory is involved or not.

You can only remember the *precipitating* cause of your trouble, and you recognize that this does not adequately explain your fear. Your *intense panic* will only make sense when the *real meaning* of it is discovered. To find that, we have to go right back into early infancy, to the time when the foundations of emotional stability are laid.

Identity

The new-born baby is quite unaware of himself as a separate individual, with his own personality and place in life. Gradually, however, he is made to feel this by other people, especially his mother. It is through her caring and tenderness that he comes to know he is a person in his own right, wanted, valued, and safe in her acceptance and her love. In such a position of security he can be 'self'-confident, and free to develop his own individuality.

Separation Anxiety

Of course, it cannot be said that the baby knows nothing of fear. There are times when he is terribly afraid — of things he does not understand, for instance — but his mother is always there to reassure him. Or is she? The greatest fear the young baby knows is that of separation anxiety or isolation. For he is completely dependent on his mother for a long time, and separation from her spells (to him) disaster, if not actual annihilation.

Yet his mother will not *always* be there, and in time the young infant has to learn to tolerate separation from her. He can do this gradually, for longer periods, until he actually comes to the point when he is glad and proud to be independent. He runs away from her – only to peep at her before long to reassure himself that she is still there! But little by little he acquires more confidence to go off on his own; and the more secure the child feels, the better able he is to be independent, and to grow up into a stable and mature adult.

Dependence

What happens, however, if the relationship offered by the mother is poor and unsatisfying? (I am not, by the way, blaming the mother here: unfortunate circumstances, such as illness, may create difficulties, and will probably have the same effect on the child as 'poor mothering'.) Does the child reject his 'unsatisfying' mother and cast her off? By no means. Unfortunately the infant cannot turn from her to other resources, for he has none. He is utterly dependent on his mother, no matter how 'unsatisfactory' she may be. She may be angry at his arrival, emotionally inhibited, or quite unable, for some other reason, to give her baby the warm, intimate, cherishing relationship he needs. But she is his only hope; he has no alternative. The result is that, far from discarding her, he remains frantically clinging to her in his state of insecurity and anxiety. He may even be so overwhelmed that he gives up in despair, and emotionally he returns to the womb.

Regressed Ego

Outwardly, he grows up. He is forced to abandon childhood. His physical and mental growth make that inevitable. But the core of his personality – his ego – is in a regressed state, living a passive existence of absolute dependence in the womb.

Here we have the root of the trouble as it has been discovered in many victims of agoraphobia. The personality of such a patient is pulled backwards by the frightened and inadequate ego, which is still clinging to the need to be a child, seeking security and protection. This need becomes the more desperate as and when the person experiences greater pressure, tension and anxiety in adult life.

Helene Deutsch found the same thing in analysing the problems of adolescent girls suffering from agoraphobia. She discovered that in most cases there was a basic, unconscious fear about growing up.

Agoraphobes are, then, defending themselves against *deep-rooted* feelings of un-safety. And in the unconscious, as a result of the patient's fixation to childhood dependence, safety = home and parents.

Here we have the reason for the desire to remain in the safety of the home. Here, too, is a *partial* explanation of the fact that some such patients can only leave home in the company of another person. It nearly always transpires that the other person represents, in the patient's unconscious, a parent-figure.[1]

Further Insights

Professor Sigmund Freud, in the course of his psycho-analytic investigations, discovered other more specific factors which sometimes lie behind agoraphobia. These relate to conflicts going on in the unconscious, about matters which have been deeply repressed since early childhood.

You must remember that the fears and anxieties of infancy are particularly devastating. The young baby feels his hold on life to be extremely tenuous, and all too easily he interprets threats and dangers as putting his whole existence in jeopardy. One thing, in particular, he must do at all costs: he must keep in with his parents, especially his mother, whose acceptance of him is vital. Without her, in his state of helpless dependence, he feels his life to be in danger.

---

[1] But see also p. 40

Conflict

The difficulty is that sooner or later in his young life he finds out that his own instincts are not always in keeping with his mother's ideas! He learns that he has to conform to certain standards of behaviour, in cleanliness and so on, if he is to keep her love and approval.

If parents are understanding and sensible, they can usually manage to win the child's co-operation without imprinting too much fear on his personality. It sometimes happens, however, that they are so anxious about the possibility of their son or daughter growing up to be perverted, or sexually depraved, that they are unduly harsh, or even cruel. If, by chance, young Tommy is caught enjoying the delights of his own body in masturbation he is thrashed until he fears for his life. Little Mary is threatened with all kinds of awful punishments if she dares to play any kind of intimate games with her small brother.

Some parents continue to exercise a terribly restrictive influence over their children for many years so that, for example, long after Mary is a grown woman she may feel it a sin to look at a man with any sort of romantic desire in her heart.

Of course such terrorizing, which is narrow, harsh and unjustified, does not do away with natural desires. The instinctual needs are still there, crying to be met. But the fear which has been instilled into the infant is also there, long after the child has grown up. Both the desire and the fear are repressed as such, but are not 'forgotten' – they still remain part of the experience, and the warfare is continued in the unconscious.

The 'Superego'

But why is it that this conflict continues into adult life, even after one has married and left the parental home? The fact is that right back in early infancy, when we first come up against the problem of 'keeping in with' our parents, on whom we are so dependent, *part of our own nature* identifies itself with the 'parent authority' – it 'sides with them', so to speak, so that we have our own *inner* 'parent authority' to keep us on the right lines. This part of our nature is what Freud called the 'superego', and it continues to exercise a controlling and restricting influence over us throughout our lives.

So the real warfare, in adult life, is not between our parents and ourselves, but between two parts of our own nature, one of which is hungry for satisfaction while the other, the superego, opposes it. This may seem strange to you. We may think that when our parents have died, or even live some distance away from us, parental approval is no longer relevant and the superego can be dismissed as redundant. Unfortunately it does not work like this. The superego became operative at the time when parental approval was felt to be *a matter of life or death* and, once established, it does not adjust itself to our independence in adult life, but remains tied to its archaic function, and influences us accordingly. (Remember, too, that we still have our 'authority figures' in adult life, and we project on to these the experience we had with our parents in infancy.)

In a person who is emotionally mature there is no problem. The rational ego exercises its judgement in regard to the influence of the superego and is not completely dominated by it.

But in cases of ego-weakness, where there is a great deal of insecurity, the superego is allowed to have full sway, amounting to a reign of terror in the unconscious. In such a state of turmoil, it is small wonder that the nervous sufferer feels exhausted.

It is also easy to see how this conflict will go on fermenting, like wine corked up tightly in a bottle, until one day a shock or trauma dislodges the 'cork', and the whole situation explodes, with consequent panic. It is in just such a way that some agoraphobic troubles develop.

A Few Illustrations

C. Edward Barker tells of one patient whom he treated:[1] a lady in middle age, who was frightened to go out, because she was terrified of fainting in the street. She had been brought up in a strict religious home, and had never married. From preliminary conversation it seemed likely that hers was a sexual problem.

During the course of her treatment she was persuaded to recapture any memories which related to sexual satisfaction of any kind. She recollected an early incident when she was assaulted — an incident which left her somewhat shocked, but also excited. There were other encounters in later life in which she enjoyed a certain degree of intimacy, but always with guilt about the circumstances.

Now, in middle age, she seemed in danger of never being satisfied sexually in a legitimate relationship. Her need was great. She was hungry for the fulfilment of a very normal and natural desire. Yet her strict upbringing made it impossible for her to seek it in a clandestine relationship.

Gradually, during her course of psychotherapy it became apparent that her fear of fainting in the street concealed a wish. It masked the desire to do that very thing — in the unconscious hope that someone might take advantage of her in her helpless faint, and give her the satisfaction for which she craved. The whole conflict was heavily repressed, but when once the fear was exposed for what it really represented, she found release.

In some cases it has been found that agoraphobia relates to a fixation at the period when the patient was learning to walk. One such patient — a young man — suffered intensely, whenever he went out, from the feeling that his legs were being pulled. Sometimes it seemed that they were running away of their own accord, and that he had no control over them.

During his course of treatment it was found that he was most severely chastised over masturbation, at the age when

[1] C. Edward Barker: *Nerves and their Cure*, Allen & Unwin.

he was learning to walk. His delight in his genitals, which he dare not express, was unconsciously transferred to pride in his walking. Later, in adult life, when the old conflict was reactivated, his terrible fear of castration (repressed since infancy) was mobilized and found expression as a fear of losing his legs. He had an underlying conflict about walking.

I remember another case of a woman who suffered from agoraphobia and a fear of crowds in general, whose phobia proved to stem from a conflict about exhibitionism.

Dr Ralph Greenson cites the case[1] of a young married woman, who could not leave the house alone, but felt safe only if her husband were with her. She also complained about her fears of dizziness, of fainting, and of becoming incontinent.

Her agoraphobia was triggered off one day when she had her hair combed by a male hairdresser — something which her father used to do when she was a little girl. Deep down she felt guilty about her inordinate love for her father; and associated with this, there was also an unconscious hostility towards her husband. In the course of her therapy she found that her fears of dizziness and of incontinence symbolized her fear of losing her moral balance and self-control.

The presence of her husband gave her an unconscious reassurance that she had not actually destroyed him, in the face of her hostility and death wishes towards him.

In all such cases it is the *conflict between desire and fear* which gives rise to the anxiety, and psycho-analysis has shown that this conflict not infrequently refers to some aspect of sexual behaviour.

The Open Street

Why should the open street become significant in these circumstances? Generally it represents, quite unconsciously, an opportunity and a temptation; and the stricter the person's moral standards the greater the conflict and anxiety.

---

[1] Dr Ralph R. Greenson: *The Technique and Practice of Psycho-analysis*, International Universities Press.

Broad streets especially seem to signify an opportunity for sexual adventure, exhibitionism, voyeurism, masturbation, or indeed any other activity about which there is underlying conflict. We can see why the company of another person may help in this connection. He, or she, represents a parent-figure to the patient — one in whose presence there is less likelihood of succumbing to the unconscious temptation. This means *safety*, for the temptation has associations in the patient's history, with danger and threats.

Incidentally, narrow streets may affect the patient in a rather different way. The patient often identifies the narrowness of the street with his own constricting emotions of anxiety and tension. So when he finds himself in a narrow street his anxiety is emphasized as he identifies himself with the narrowness of it. (Alternatively, an agoraphobe may feel 'trapped' upon entering a narrow street.)

Obsession

Almost any type of neurotic conflict may betray itself in symptoms of agoraphobia. Obsessive patients, for example, may fear the street as a place where they can be caught, with no-one to shield them from punishment. The phobia is then masking a guilt complex.

One of my patients, with obsessive symptoms, has said on more than one occasion that on finding himself in a crowded store he has broken out in a cold sweat. There was a feeling of un-safety which he could not understand, and his one thought was to get out as quickly as possible.

Another patient obsessed by guilt could only venture out in the company of his wife. Analysis showed clearly that she represented to him the mother whom he hated as a baby, and indeed had 'destroyed' at that time in his imagination. The presence of this 'mother-figure' in the person of his wife, was an unconscious reassurance that he had not, in fact, destroyed her.

Let me remind you again that this sort of problem must be looked at in the context of infantile experience, where it belongs, to appreciate the intensity of the anxiety.

You can see from all this that behind the precipitating factor in agoraphobia there lies, deeply buried, some anxiety or conflict from the earliest days of childhood. The agoraphobia is a distortion. The real fear is projected on to the fear of the street. This is why it appears so illogical. It can only be seen in perspective when viewed in the right context – in babyhood. At that age feelings were a matter of life and death, and panic was terrifying. One was left helpless in one's anxiety, and could deal with it in only one way – by repressing it.

CHAPTER FIVE

AGORAPHOBIA AND CLAUSTROPHOBIA

So many agoraphobics suffer also from symptoms of claustrophobia that I thought it might be helpful if I were to devote one chapter to the link between these two emotional disorders. They appear to be contradictory, but in actual fact they are often found to be reverse sides of the same coin, as in the following case.

The patient, a young man, had been the only child of a well-meaning but possessive mother, who gave him 'smother-love' instead of the real mother love he needed. It was as though his life was being stifled, and it was hardly surprising that in later years he suffered from claustrophobia.

If he ventured into a lift, for instance, he would panic at once and get out at the first opportunity, sweating and trembling like a leaf. Being in such an enclosed space unconsciously mobilized the old fear of 'suffocation' which was a legacy from his childhood.

At the same time, however, he showed symptoms of agoraphobia which were traceable to his state of dependence. He had reached manhood still being looked after by his over-protective mother, and was quite unable to stand on his own feet. If he went out alone he felt unsafe. Unconsciously he was still in need of protection, even though he was also in fear of being smothered by that same protection. What a dilemma! It was only after bringing the cause of his trouble to light and encouraging the growth of his own ego that he was freed from his phobias and helped towards a position of emotional maturity.

Flight

Phobias are, of course, a form of flight, and this is an instinctive reaction to danger. As little children, if we are frightened we run *away from* the danger, *to* safety (mother's protection). All phobic states constitute a flight from danger to a position of safety. The agoraphobic patient sees the external world as a threat – and hence the flight to the safety of home. The claustrophobe fears any situation in which he feels stifled, and hence his flight to a position of freedom.

We may also note, in passing, that something amounting to an *obsession* concerning the source of safety establishes itself in both cases. I remember the case of a young lady who only felt safe with her fiancé. One day they were involved in a bad accident in the car, while he was driving, but her obsessive need to cling to him for safety remained, quite unshaken by what had happened.

Trapped!

Now one feature of both phobias becomes apparent – the need for a way of escape; flight demands it. The 'don't fence me in' attitude of the claustrophobe is easy to understand. But why does the agoraphobic patient *also* have a fear of being 'trapped'? 'Surely', you may say, 'one should not feel trapped in the outside world!' But this is just what such a patient *does* feel. If he is on a bus or train he feels trapped because he is not free to get off at any one second; if he is in any crowded situation – a busy store, or street, a theatre or football ground – he feels trapped by the people about him.

He feels hemmed in and caught in a position of danger, without any possibility of making an escape back to the safety of home. But why is this fear of being trapped so important? How does it arise in the first place? Again this takes us back to early life, to a very basic factor in our emotional development. For those who are interested to understand this, I will try to explain as simply as I can something of what is involved.

The Schizoid Factor

Let me at once reassure you about the term 'schizoid'. It does *not* mean 'schizophrenic', but refers to the regressed state which I described in the previous chapter.

You will remember that we saw relationship to be of paramount importance to the development of our personalities. It is now recognized that the key to psychological development lies in the relationship of a person to his environment. In particular, it is from relationship with other *people* that we develop a sense of our own personality.

What happens if the tiny infant cannot get a satisfactory relationship with the people in his world? He grows up with a sense of unreality; he becomes introverted and withdrawn. If good relationships are just not forthcoming and the anxiety becomes too great, then he tries to deny this basic need. Outwardly he adopts an aloof, unemotional attitude, which avoids *feeling* as far as possible. But inwardly his need of a love relationship is desperate.

Such a person finds himself in conflict – hungry for love and close relationship, yet afraid of entering into any such situation. He may even feel that his own hungry need will destroy the love that does come his way.

The first relationship we know as infants is one of *identification* (with mother, of course). It is only later that we make relationships objectively with her and with other people. But to go from one to the other is quite a big step in emotional development. There is a transitional state in which the individual is torn between the urge to become independent and the fear of abandoning the safety of the identification relationship.

Dr Harry S. Guntrip, perhaps the greatest authority on the schizoid state at the present time, relates the dream of an agoraphobic patient,[1] which clearly shows the conflict between the need to be dependent and the need to become *in*dependent.

[1] H. Guntrip: *Personality Structure and Human Interaction*, Hogarth Press.

The patient, an agoraphobic, dreamed of being in prison. A young man gave him a file to cut through the bars, but he said that it was unnecessary as the doors were not locked. Asked why he did not escape, he replied: 'See how dangerous it is out there! How would I be if I found myself out there all alone?' He then became aware of his mother, the jailoress, standing behind him – though she was not holding him. He was free to go if he had so wished.

The patient had previously had many dreams of trying to break out of prison, but in this one we clearly see his ambivalence. He wanted to be free – yet he dare not leave the 'safety' of the prison.

Thus the schizoid patient maintains what Dr Guntrip calls an 'in and out' position. He cannot commit himself to close relationship, yet he is equally afraid of becoming independent. He wants to keep both avenues open, so he tries to 'sit on the fence' and maintain a compromise position of non-committal.

Indecision

Here we can see an explanation of the indecision which characterizes phobic patients. The making of any decision symbolizes, unconsciously, the great underlying decision which the patient cannot take, the one concerning his relationships, so vital to his life.

Yet another reason why this character trait is shared by victims of both these phobias lies in the fact that some decisions are not easily reversed. This means, again, a fear of being 'trapped' – of burning one's boats in certain directions, or shutting the door on one alternative. The claustrophobe may feel this as the fear of shutting himself *in* – committing himself to something from which he cannot escape. The agoraphobe may feel it as a fear of shutting himself *out* – of leaving the 'home' position, or *status quo*, without the possibility of returning.

In all these cases it is the *symbolic* significance of decision-making which presents the difficulty to the phobic patient. But in any case the making of decisions requires some degree of independence and maturity, the ability to take the initiative. The person who is suffering from ego-weakness, or who is withdrawn and introverted, is bound to find this difficult.

Isolation Dread

One feature which is common to both agoraphobia and claustrophobia is the fear of isolation. Again, it may seem strange to speak of isolation dread in regard to a phobia about going into the street where there are people about. You may think this is just the opposite of isolation anxiety. Let me explain.

You will recognize, I am sure, from your own experience, that 'isolation' is not the same thing as 'being on your own'. You may feel more truly isolated in a busy street or on a crowded bus, then when you are alone in the familiar surroundings of your own home.

Dr R.D. Laing tells of a patient who felt rejected and insignificant.[1] She could be on her own, as long as there was no sense of isolation or of being ignored. But she felt *most* insecure in a crowded street, because she became very conscious of the crowds passing her by, without noticing her. It brought to the surface her feelings of unreality, and her unsureness about her own identity.

Again we have to look to very early infancy to see the true significance of isolation anxiety. As I have said, we exist only in relationship with the world about us. *Complete* isolation carries the ultimate threat of non-existence, not only because of our utter helplessness to exist by ourselves physically, but also because our personality demands that we exist in relationship. We need people to be aware of us (that is, we need to feel of some significance to other people) if we are to realize our own identity.

This isolation anxiety manifests itself in claustrophobic fears, for if the patient is shut in, he is also shut off from communication. But a similar feeling attaches to being

[1] Dr R.D. Laing: *The Divided Self*, Tavistock.

'imprisoned' or 'trapped' in the depersonalizing atmosphere of a crowded shop or street. Equally, the fear of open spaces may be another expression of isolation dread.

Unreality

Any situation in which one is cut off from the 'safety of home' can produce isolation dread, and if this anxiety becomes too great the patient may defend himself against the terror by 'negating' himself. He cuts out feeling, and resorts to a state of depersonalization. His contact with the external world emphasizes his needs and his anxiety, so he withdraws himself emotionally from this environment which is felt to be so dangerous. The feeling of unreality he experiences in so doing only adds to his anxiety, of course, and is no solution.

Dr Guntrip describes[1] how another of his patients, a young woman of nineteen, was chronically agoraphobic. At the same time, she felt *claustrophobic* whenever she went into a big store. Her problem was investigated by analytic treatment, and this revealed the connection between the two. She felt so overwhelmed and helpless in the crowded shop, that her only 'defence' was one of depersonalization and schizoid withdrawal. This involved a terrible feeling of unreality and lack of contact with everything and everybody, and it was this that led eventually to her chronic agoraphobia.

[1] Dr Harry S. Guntrip: *Schizoid Phenomena, Object Relations and the Self*, Hogarth.

PART II
THE WAY FORWARD

CHAPTER SIX

FREEDOM FROM FEAR

In this second part of the book I am going to explain to you various ways in which your trouble may be overcome. Not every patient responds in the same manner to a particular type of approach. The method which has proved helpful to one patient may do little for another.

I have heard of patients seeking help from the practice of yoga, and from treatment by acupuncture: with what results I do not know. Shock treatment has been used to cure some phobias, but I have no personal knowledge of long-term agoraphobic patients cured by this method. Again, the effectiveness of this form of treatment varies greatly from one patient to another.

Some patients have found help from group therapy – but there are serious difficulties in the way of agoraphobic patients getting to such groups, and not all people take kindly to this particular type of therapy.

I know of one patient with a deep religious faith who found great help through the ministry of the laying-on-of-hands. But no one method can be guaranteed to cure all patients. What I do want to emphasize is that agoraphobia can be cured, indeed *has* been cured, in different ways.

First I want to ask the question: should one try to *erase* the fear, or should one *live through it*, in order to overcome it? The two methods of therapy which I shall describe in some detail in succeeding chapters are based on the latter assumption – that the only way to overcome fear is to live through it.

There are other forms of treatment, however, which seek

to dispel the fear, either by encouraging right thinking, or by the help of drugs. Certainly the promise of curing the trouble without the awful experience of living through one's fear sounds attractive. Let us look at these possibilities briefly.

Auto-suggestion

One school of thought aims at removing fear predominantly by the encouragement of positive thinking. It is largely a matter of auto-suggestion. If you suggest to your mind that you will be afraid, you will suffer accordingly. But if you suggest to yourself that you will *not* be afraid, you are much more likely to be serene and confident.

I must admit that I support whole-heartedly the encouragement of positive thinking and affirmation. Indeed, without it any form of therapy is likely to fail. But is it sufficient in itself to effect a sound and permanent cure?

Positive thinking may certainly help the patient to take the first steps outside the house, and to acquire greater confidence in time. But what of the sudden alarm, the unexpected shock, which could so easily re-sensitize the patient? Only if the person has persevered faithfully and successfully with auto-suggestion techniques over a very long period is it likely that he, or she, will be sufficiently stable to cope with the *unexpected anxiety* without getting into a panic once more.

Hypnotherapy

This is another method of removing fear, and you may think it could be the ideal answer. Some patients have found great help from such treatment. A recent newsletter from 'The Open Door' organization mentions one elderly woman who had been agoraphobic for more than seven years, who finally managed to join her family in Australia after a three-months' course of hypnotherapy.

It would be wrong, however, for me to give you false hopes and make rash promises about the likelihood of success if you decide to try this method. In the first place, not all people are suitable subjects for hypnosis. Secondly, it is most essential that the hypnotist is properly trained, not only in hypnosis but also in depth psychology, if he is to give effective help which is well-founded.

It is also true that psychotherapists used to employ hypnosis more than they do nowadays: they find, on the whole, that therapy is more soundly based when it involves the conscious will of the patient. Results tend to be less permanent when induced by hypnosis.

Certainly you should be on your guard against charlatans, who practise hypnosis without fully understanding the patient's condition and his deepest needs.

Drugs

Another alternative is the use of fear-removing drugs. In my opinion there are many disadvantages to this form of treatment. Drugs may be helpful as an aid to relaxation in the early stages of desensitization, but to depend on them for maintaining emotional stability is, to my mind, only a second-best substitute for real therapy. It is possible that the drugs must be continued over a long time, or for ever, unless the patient is ready to wean himself from their use. And trying to break away from the drug habit may, in any case, prove just as painful as the more radical forms of therapy which I will describe.

Again, can one be sure that there will be no harmful side-effects, if the drugs are taken over a long time? Is it certain that they will retain their effectiveness, or will the patient require stronger drugs as time goes on?

It can also be argued that a sense of fear is necessary for our protection, in certain circumstances. Will the drug make the patient less alert and alive to real dangers if and when they arise? I am firmly of the opinion that the best way to conquer fear is to face it.

Desensitization

The first chapter of this book showed us how a sudden shock or unexpected trauma can sensitize a person, so that he or she acquires a most appalling dread of being caught again in a state of panic.

One method of cure now being used extensively in the Behaviour Therapy departments of certain hospitals is known as 'desensitization' or 'relaxation' treatment.

Exponents of behaviour therapy techniques, of whom Professor Eysenck is one of the most well-known, see phobic reactions merely as emotional habits which have been learnt. They are faulty, maladjusted habits, inappropriate (in intensity at least) to the situation. The cure lies, therefore, in re-conditioning the patient to new habits. It is based upon the idea that the patient should be encouraged to face up to his fear, and then to overcome it in easy stages, so that he learns a habit of confidence.

When We Were Young

This cure has sound psychological principles behind it, for it uses the very methods by which we naturally overcome our fears as children — by doing the thing we fear, over and over again.

The little girl, for instance, who shrieks when her daddy throws her into the air in case he should let her fall, will ask him to do it again — and again. She is putting her fears to the test, and finding they are without foundation. In an earlier chapter I reminded you of how the toddler does the same thing when he is overcoming separation anxiety — leaving his mother, and then running back to her for reassurance before running off on his own again.

We master our fears in this way throughout our life. You may have learned to swim, as I did, by pushing off from the bottom of the sea, and making one stroke before putting your toe down again. Then you tried once more, and made two strokes. Gradually you did a few more, until you found that the water really would bear you up, and your fear subsided.

Desensitization works along similar lines. The patient faces up to his fear in stages, and tests it out very gradually, until it loses its hold over him.

The Habit of Fear

The technique of desensitization is based on the fact that a phobia of any kind is an emotional reaction which has become an ingrained habit. Indeed, we might go further and say it has become an *automatic response* to a particular situation. Confront the acrophobe with the view from the Post Office tower, and he will react spontaneously with a fit of terror. Put an aerophobe into an aeroplane and, even before it gets off the ground, you will get a response as sure as a reflex action — panic.

So with your agoraphobia. You have become conditioned to a fear of going out. It is now an automatic reaction, and every time you give into the fear you are strengthening its hold on you.

The Technique

Desensitization treatment is given at various London hospitals and also in some provincial ones. The method may vary a little according to the views and experience of the therapist. A patient has described the procedure followed by a psychiatrist at one London teaching hospital.

The patient is taken into a room where he is encouraged to relax. The therapist then breaks down the phobic situation into different parts. For example, in the case of agoraphobia these could include: walking down the path, going through the gate, walking to the pillarbox three houses away, crossing the road to the bus stop, boarding the bus, and so on. Then slowly and carefully he exposes the patient to the fear experienced at each stage. This is first done in imaginative work in the consulting room. The patient goes through the situation in fantasy, indicating at each point how severe his feeling of panic is. For if he really enters into this imaginatively, even the *thought* of going down the road will arouse panic.

He numbers his reactions from one to ten — ten representing the state of complete terror. He may say 'three' or 'four' for 'walking down the path', and it may well shoot up to 'eight' or 'nine' for 'going through the gate'.

During another session the therapist instructs the patient in the art of complete relaxation, and helps him to practise it until he can relax very readily.

Now the real therapy begins. At succeeding sessions the therapist takes the patient, again in imagination, through the different parts of the situation, beginning with the one with the lowest rating of fear — perhaps 'going down the path'. The patient is fearful as he imagines leaving his front door and going down to the gate. But he is encouraged to relax, and as he does so he finds that his fear lessens, dropping from, say, three, to two and then one. When he can fantasy doing that one small thing with little or no fear, the therapist takes him on to the next.

The same process is repeated with the increasingly fearful aspects of the situation. When sufficient mastery of the fear has been established at each step, in imagination, then and only then, the patient is asked to go out, and actually face up to the experience which terrified him and for which he sought help.

It sometimes happens, of course, that a patient finds it difficult to enter imaginatively into fantasy work of this kind. He, or she, may be too tense, or have only limited powers of concentration. In such cases some psychiatrists use a drug to help relaxation, and so make the work a little easier.

Effectiveness

The therapists using this method claim that about eighty per cent of their patients receive substantial help from this form of treatment, though they do not assert that the cure is perfect. Many patients learn to *tolerate* the experience, rather than to enjoy it. They can, however, find sufficient release from their fear to live much more happily.

Agoraphobia, which has always been one of the most stubborn phobias to cure, has been treated quite successfully by this method. In an article in *The Daily Telegraph* colour magazine some time ago a fifty-nine-year-old former general sales manager described how he had been helped in this way.

His previous work had taken him on long and frequent journeys around the country, but then he developed agoraphobia and for ten years was reduced to doing some work at home, being quite unable to leave the house.

In his desensitization treatment he was encouraged to imagine he was going out of the gate, then to the end of the road, and so on. He tells how he eventually went outside and began to conquer his fears in actual experience, in the same way as he had practised in the course of his treatment. At the time of writing he could drive up to forty miles in the car, and go into the centre of the town where he lived, without panic.

Support and Encouragement

As you can see, desensitization does not offer an easy or instantaneous release from fear. What it does offer is encouragement to face the fear, first in the supportive and relaxing atmosphere created by the therapist, and then in the real world outside.

In the next chapter I am going to tell you how you can help yourself by means of desensitization, bearing in mind the fact that by the very nature of your difficulty, you may not be able to get to a trained therapist for help.

CHAPTER SEVEN

SELF-HELP IN DESENSITIZATION

Inevitably there are very many agoraphobic patients who, by reason of their emotional condition, just cannot get to a hospital or therapist. If they are to find relief at all, it must be by some method which enables them to help themselves. Fortunately, desensitization does lend itself to self-help reasonably well. Dr Claire Weekes, a consultant physician in Sydney, Australia, has done a great deal of work with such patients and claims considerable success.

Four Principles
Dr Weeks describes her method as having four basic principles.[1] She calls them: (1) facing (2) accepting (3) floating and (4) letting time pass. Her advice is:

(1) *Do not try to force yourself to forget your fear – face up to it, acknowledge its existence.* Now this is surely sound advice, for you will never solve a problem if you are trying to forget it exists.

(2) *Do not fight against the fear, but accept it.* In this way you will not perpetuate and aggravate things by piling on what Dr Weekes calles 'second fear', that is, the 'What if . . . ' and 'Supposing . . . '

(3) *Do not tense yourself against the fear, which will only increase stress, but rather let it have its way for the time being.* Go with the feeling; let it pass through you, as it were, until it has spent itself.

(4) *Do not be discouraged because you are not cured in a few days, or even weeks.* Do not spend too much time in introspection and disappointment at your failures. Be prepared for the process to take time.

This last point is important. Many patients are far too hard on themselves. They forget that the wrong emotional habits

[1] Dr Claire Weekes: *Peace from Nervous Suffering*, Angus & Robertson.

have been going on over a long time, and cannot be wiped out straight away. Do not set a time limit on your recovery, and give up if you do not make it. Be patient with yourself, and let time pass without worrying over it: or you will be re-sensitizing yourself to worry all over again!

The Step-by-Step Approach

So much for the basic principles. What are you to do to help yourself in practice, in this desensitization process? Follow, if you like, the technique I have described in the previous chapter, as far as you are able.

a. Face up to the fears of the situation which frightens you, by breaking it down into parts, as suggested, and feeling the *severity* of the fear at each point.

b. Now practise the art of relaxation. Lie on a comfortable bed and let all your muscles go completely loose. Be aware of this relaxation in every part of your body. For example, concentrate on your toes, ankles, knees, thighs and hips. Then on your shoulders, arms, wrists, fingers and thumbs. Finally your back, tummy, chest, nape of the neck, jaw, facial muscles and brow. Feel that *every* part of you is· relaxed.

c. When you are completely relaxed physically, allow yourself to relax mentally. Let all thoughts of duties and responsibilities go. Let all worries go: *at this moment* you have nothing to worry about. You are safe and secure. A little auto-suggestion will probably help you here. Affirm quietly to yourself that with every breath you take you are becoming more relaxed. As you breathe in more deeply, you are becoming more deeply relaxed. Practise this art of relaxation until you have really mastered it.

d. Now you are ready to imagine the situation which you fear, recognizing the fear and letting it have its way, yet relaxing in the knowledge that you are safe. Fear cannot harm you, so don't be afraid of feeling it. Follow the method I have described in the previous chapter. As you imagine, say, walking down the path to the gate, *let the feeling of fear come;* but *relax at the same time* in the way you have practised, until you feel the fear gradually subsiding.

e. When you have mastered the fear in the *least* frightening part of the situation you can go on to deal with the more difficult aspects of it. It is important for you to go right through the situation in detail, even to the most terrifying incidents that could happen.

Face the Worst, in Imagination

Are you imagining going for a bus ride? Then go through all

the trifling things which might unnerve you. See yourself being jostled as you get on. Hear the conductor's voice saying 'Pass along the bus, please' — the last thing you want to do! Imagine, if you like, the glare of the woman next to you, as she bundles all her big parcels on to her lap to give you a seat. Perhaps you find you have only a note for a small fare. The conductor glowers at you and murmurs something under his breath. Use your imagination to go through all the possible emergencies you can think of — the things which you, personally, would find unnerving. Maybe, for example, you see the bus still crowded as you reach your destination, and you have to squeeze past several standing passengers to get to the door.

In fact go, in fantasy, through the worst that could possibly happen, and face up to the fear at each point. But remember that as you feel the panic *you also allow yourself to relax*, and you will become aware that the panic is actually falling away from you.

Relaxation Is All-important

A great deal of the success of this form of therapy depends on the element of relaxation. This is why some psychiatrists use drugs to help patients who are very tense.

So many patients say: 'I just *can't* relax'. I expect you have read articles and booklets on the art of relaxation. I wonder if you have *seriously* tried to follow the suggestions contained in them, whether you have really *persevered* with the techniques and exercises recommended. It is so easy to make a half-hearted attempt, and then give up. I know it is difficult, if you have been living on your strain and stress, to believe that anything else is possible for you. But a lot is at stake, so do be encouraged to persevere.

Now For the Reality

When you have mastered your fear imaginatively from the safety of your room, you are ready to do the same thing in the real world outside. If you have been quite unable to leave the house at all, go from your back door to the dustbin. If you feel the panic starting, don't rush back to the house, but *relax* until the fear gradually falls away from you.

Repeat that same little experiment until you can do it with very little fear; then try to go a little further — cross the path to the garage. When that ceases to terrify you, try to go as far as the gate; later you can go outside the gate and along to the pillar-box a few yards away. Continue in this way until you can get to the bus-stop and board a bus for a short journey.

(Of course, despite my suggestions for imaginative work, you should actually make things as easy as you can for yourself the first time — choose a time when the bus will not be crowded, and see that you have some small change for the fare.)

I can imagine you saying that you doubt very much whether you can really do this. It sounds too difficult. Remember that others have felt as you do, but have had the courage to try, and have found considerable release by following this method. You can do the same — if you really want to.

That last phrase is important, and is not so harsh and unfeeling as it sounds. I will explain more to you about this in Chapter Ten.

Persevere Despite the Fear

Of course it will not be easy. If you give up as soon as you panic, you will be back in your prison again. It is only by facing the fear, and living through it, realizing that the *fear itself cannot harm you*, that you will gradually lose your anxiety and find freedom.

Do not wait until you think you can go down the road without fear, or you may wait for ever. The important thing to remember is that you can do it *despite the fear* you may feel. So make a start *now*. If you have already faced the fear, in your fantasy, and felt it subside, when you step out into the garden or the street you can expect your panic to be less than it has been. But don't expect to be *completely* fearless when you go out, or you will quickly be disappointed and give up. Your fear can and will subside if you allow it to.

(You have already learned this in your imaginative work in your room.)

It is a case of experiencing the fear again and again, accepting it rather than letting it upset you, until you become almost impervious to it. It will cease to bother you, and become irrelevant. It has been said that there is no worry so small but it will grow if you feed it with attention. The same is true of fear, and this is what has been happening to you. You have worried about your fear. You have fed it with attention. Fear can be 'starved to death' if one accepts the fact that it is there, and then goes on living in spite of it. As I said this takes some courage and determination. Yet this is the way forward.

CHAPTER EIGHT

IS THERE AN EASIER WAY?

You may well feel that the desensitization method I have described involves too much discipline, too much concentrated and consistent effort, for you to be able to manage on your own, and perhaps you cannot leave the house to go to a trained therapist.

'Is there a simpler solution?' you ask. I do appreciate how you feel, especially if your problem is not merely a specific limitation, but one of general nervous tension which seems to bar you from concentrating on imaginative work.

Let us be realistic. Desensitization involves exposing yourself to fear, in order to master it. It has something in common with the medical technique of immunization, in which you take a small dose of the illness in order to build up your power to withstand its onslaught and overcome it. You do have one choice, however, in the present case. Either you expose yourself to the fear gradually, by a planned recovery method, or you take the bull by the horns and see what happens.

Flooding

A more controversial form of desensitization than the one I have described, is known as 'flooding'. It consists of pushing the patient into the very situation he dreads, and letting him 'sweat it out' until he gradually discovers that there is nothing to fear. In the case of agoraphobia, the person would be taken out into a public park or some similar situation, and left there for hours on end until he learned to bear it. (He would, of course, be kept under supervision.) There can be few psychiatrists, I think, who would expose their patients to this form of treatment.

Taking the Plunge

There *are* people, however, who have had the courage to jump in at the deep end, with only a little preparation, and have found it work. Not long ago an article in a Sunday newspaper told of a sixty-two year old widow — we will call her Mrs A. — who had been a prisoner in her own home for eleven years. To step outside the door put her in a terrible panic. Neighbours collected her pension and did her shopping for her. Meanwhile she spent her leisure hours doing jig-saw puzzles, watching television and listening to records.

She had been a foster-mother for many years, and a former foster-child, now married and living thirty-four miles away, had often invited her to stay. But it was quite impossible for her to contemplate making the journey — or so it seemed. One more invitation came and Mrs A. decided to make, as she put it, a 'once-for-all effort'.

The travelling was arranged to make it as easy as possible for her. A friend and his family took her in their van. She managed the journey reasonably well, with the children to occupy her attention. Then one day, while she was away, her hostess said: 'Put your coat on — we're going shopping.' After spending some time in the shops, they went into a restaurant for a meal. Further outings followed, during her short stay of six days, and the fact that someone was with her helped to make it easier. But the real test came when she went home — *alone*, by bus. Mrs. A writes: 'We came up the M1 — the first time I had seen a motorway. The day was dull and the scenery ordinary but I began to enjoy it — seeing the trees and fields, and realizing that *my fear was fading*. Only when I got home did it begin to sink in that I had beaten the fear. I cannot describe how dreadful it has been. Just to step outside the door put me in terrible panic. Now it is almost like being born again. I can go out *without a qualm*, catch buses and do my own shopping.'

A Struggle

It is only fair to say, however, that not everyone who has tried this way has found it so easy. Mrs B., writing in a weekly paper, makes it clear that for her it has been and still is, a struggle all the way.

Her agoraphobia followed a period of physical illness and nervous breakdown. She decided she must fight against the phobia if she were to regain any sort of normal life, and it seemed easier for her to venture out when it was dark and the street was deserted. With the help and encouragement of a very understanding husband, she took the plunge at ten o'clock one night. She went one hundred yards down the road, and came back sobbing. She did not force herself to do this every night, but as often as she could she braved the night air, gradually covering greater distances.

That was nine years ago, and she continued to 'persevere despite the fear' — a good motto for agoraphobics! It has been uphill all the way for Mrs B. But she did improve sufficiently for her to take her daughter to school, and do her own shopping. She could go back to the church to which she belonged, and just occasionally she could manage a visit to a restaurant or a theatre.

Her article makes it plain, however, that the battle still rages; she says she has learned to live a tightrope existence. She is still unable to travel on buses or trains, and there is a constant strain whenever she goes out. She suffers still from rising panic and claustrophobia in public meetings of any kind, and if a minor illness keeps her indoors for a day or so, the resultant setback is hard to bear.

Obviously this is not a cure. This courageous lady has learned to live with agoraphobia, and none but her close friends realize her difficulties. She has, by her determination, made life a little easier for her family as well as for herself, but it is not the perfect answer.

Perhaps one clue to Mrs B's difficulty lies in her own phrase 'I knew I had to *fight*'. In actual fact, the important thing about any attempt at desensitization is to learn to *relax*. As I have said, this is one of the main points about doing imaginative work *before* you venture out into the street. By learning to relax in your fantasy work at home, you will more easily apply the same technique when you go outside to put it into practice.

You may wonder why Mrs B. found it so difficult, while Mrs A. seems to have found 'instant release'. Why does it work for one and not for another? The answer to this probably lies in the different temperaments and backgrounds of the two people. As I said earlier, no two people respond to the same form of therapy in exactly the same way. You must also remember that Mrs B. had to contend with the after-effects of a *general* physical and nervous breakdown (including, incidentally, a period of depression following a miscarriage while she was fighting her agoraphobia).

Planned Recovery

Perhaps you have tried taking the plunge, with such 'disastrous' results, in terms of panic and upset, that you dare not try again. Yet you may also feel that the imaginative preparation I described in the previous chapter is beyond you. Then try a simpler form of planned recovery.

If you have just one friend who will help you, so much the better, especially if you live alone. It can be very wearying and disheartening to go battling on, with no one to share your minor victories and give you encouragement when you might be tempted to give up. It is also true that trying to go out for a short walk 'just for the sake of it' can seem very pointless. A friend may help to make your short 'outings' more purposeful.

If she lives close at hand you may get to the point of making a daily visit to her house for coffee, or for tea. You will no doubt find some way of repaying her kindness as you are able. Don't be too embarrassed or independent to accept such help; I am sure your friend will be just as thrilled as you are about your progress, and she will get great satisfaction from having had a hand in your recovery.

Perhaps your only contact can be by way of letter or telephone, but it will still mean quite a lot to you to be able to share your ups and downs with someone else. If you do live alone, it may also be a good idea to keep a diary. If you cannot report on your progress to another person, at least you can record it here. It will enable you to look back after a while, too, and see how far you have come. But remember what I said in Chapter Seven about not setting your sights *too* high, or putting a time limit on your recovery. Don't be dismayed by setbacks, but accept them as being only temporary. You can and will recover from them if you are patient with yourself.

No one is in a position to *promise* a complete cure to any patient, where emotional troubles are concerned, and agoraphobia is no exception. Some patients improve, but continue to find life a struggle at times. Others, whose release is more complete, become so overjoyed that they take a delight in going out as much as possible. Such a patient may become quite a globe-trotter, making up for lost time!

So much depends on the patient's personality, early life and upbringing, environmental stresses, and the deep underlying cause of the phobia. Nevertheless, be on your guard against making this an excuse to remain in your unhappy state. You may have been 'imprisoned' in your home for many years, but you do not have to make it a 'life sentence'. Let the experience of others encourage you. It shows you what can be done, and it is good for you to accept the challenge that it presents to you.

The Final Answer?

The psychiatrists who advocate desensitization do not maintain that it is a complete cure. It enables the patient to cope with a situation which had previously caused him to panic, and from which he has consistently withdrawn himself. The fact is, of course, that a treatment which does not go to the *root* cause of the panic is stopping short of what is needed for a complete cure.

Dr Weekes, who writes somewhat disparagingly of analytic techniques, admits that patients who have improved considerably by desensitization may, years later, have recurrences of the panic and need to repeat the treatment in order to desensitize themselves once more.

The only possible solution if a patient wishes to remove the *cause* of the panic completely is to trace it to its original repressed source in the unconscious.

We have seen that the panic is out of all proportion to the facts of the case. It is irrational as it stands, and can be explained only in the context of the original emotional trauma from which it sprang.

The *true* nature of the fear has been hidden and distorted by the forces of repression. Likewise, the *emotional need associated with the fear* is unrevealed by desensitization techniques.

Dr Weekes says that exposing a childhood cause of agoraphobia rarely helps in the cure. It is quite true that *merely to expose* the cause will produce only limited benefit. Analysis may be interesting, but only in rare cases will that alone bring release. It can, and does happen in odd instances, but normally analysis must be accompanied by a positive therapy involving re-education if the patient is to receive the maximum benefit.

What Is Meant by Cure?

The question must be asked: 'What is the patient seeking? What does he, or she, mean by "being cured"?'

Take the case of the lady mentioned in Chapter Four, who was afraid of fainting in the street. It was found that her fear was traceable to inhibitions and conflict concerning her natural need of a close, intimate relationship. Suppose she managed, by desensitization treatment, to overcome her fear of fainting in the street — could it be said that she was cured? Admittedly, she would know great release, and those who treated her *would* pronounce her cured. They would have dealt with the presenting symptom — agoraphobia — but *not* with the needs of her personality.

The behaviour therapists describe phobic reactions as habits which have been wrongly learned; they do not tell us why that came to be so. We are told that the cause of the trouble is irrelevant; the thing to do is to cure it. Now the point is that when the real cause of the trouble is found – when we see *why* the habit of panic has established itself – we come upon the *deeper* need of the patient, and can deal with that accordingly. It is a question of whether one wants to cure a symptom, or heal a personality.

In the case of this lady, the desperate frustration would still be there and would probably find some other outlet, just as depressing. How much more fulfilling her life will be if the underlying inhibitions are brought to the surface and dealt with. The agoraphobia will be cured at the same time, of course, as it will in any case lose its force when once the cause of it has been exposed. The patient can then more easily be re-conditioned to the habit of going out instead of staying in.

If the agoraphobic patient is seeking only to overcome his fear of going out, then desensitization may work wonders, and enable him to live a much happier life. But such treatment does not get down to the basic problem of understanding and meeting the needs of, for example, the tiny immature ego, still clinging inwardly to dependence on mother. Psychotherapy uncovers this, the real need, and seeks to meet it.

Conflict Still There

The man who can go out only in the company of his wife might be encouraged to overcome that problem, but would that alone deal with his underlying anxiety about repressed death wishes against his mother?

The young woman whose agoraphobia is a defence against exhibitionism will still be held in the grip of this conflict (unless it is brought to light and dealt with) even though she is enabled to conquer her fear of walking in the street. A conflict which no longer expresses itself in one form will continue its disruptive work and is likely to find expression in some other way, unless it is treated.

Wholeness

Those who say that agoraphobes are cured by desensitization alone, judge from the results in terms of the ability to go out. Psychotherapists are concerned with the wholeness of the personality. Without the use of analytic techniques the underlying cause of the phobia – the conflict or ego-weakness – is not recognized; neither is the basic emotional need of the patient met.

It may be argued, of course, that when the fear of going out is dealt with, there is a great deal of improvement in self-confidence and stability of the personality generally. I would certainly not dispute this. The ability to live a normal life once more, the freedom from fear, and from feelings of guilt and failure – these, and many other factors, help a great deal towards re-integration of the personality.

I am, however, bound to say again that dealing with the fear of panic, without looking for the root cause of the terror does not resolve the intra-psychic conflict, nor does it meet the deep, emotional needs of the person which have not, in any case, been brought to the surface.

One cannot know the true extent of a person's need, merely by combating the fear. As someone has said: 'It's like trying to cure measles by treating the spots'. It is treating a symptom, while the illness remains. It is liable to break out in some other form, but in any case it is debilitating.

My own attitude, therefore, would be not *merely* to cure the fear of panic and so enable the patient to go about more freely, but to help him to *go forward to wholeness*. Perhaps, as a practising psychotherapist, I am biased in my views – but then I have had, in the course of my training, a full training analysis. No one could therefore convince me that analytic psychotherapy has little to offer. My own experience is quite undeniable.

Investment in Happiness

It is true, however, that this form of treatment is lengthy and also expensive. It must be regarded, in fact, as an investment: an investment in future happiness and fulfilment, in emotional stability and in freedom, not just from the fear which is a *symptom* of intra-psychic 'dis-ease', but from the disease itself.

When that is achieved, then as one patient recently remarked in my hearing: 'It is like being born again, almost literally. I am a new person'. This is wholeness, and this is what I would wish for every nervous sufferer.

I have pointed out, however, that desensitization lends itself more easily to self-help, and as a cure for the fear of going out it is extremely valuable.

Perhaps I should say that it need not be a case of either . . or. Both techniques have a place in helping patients. Analytic psychotherapy need not preclude the practising of desensitization techniques. Indeed, in some cases these are necessary if the patient is to get to the therapist at all. But the analytic therapist will not be content to enable the patient to go out. He will meet the greater challenge: of helping him, or her, to become emancipated from the underlying conflicts, inhibition, and state of dependence which otherwise will continue to exercise a backward pull on the personality, and rob the patient of a great deal of happiness and fulfilment.

In a word, he aims for 'wholeness'.

CHAPTER NINE

ANALYTIC PSYCHOTHERAPY

Bearing in mind the *deeper* causes of phobias, (see Chapters Four and Five) some patients prefer to get down to the original root of the trouble, by means of psychotherapy.

In this case it is preferable to have the help of a trained psychotherapist, though it is possible to obtain some insights into your problem yourself, if you are prepared to take some trouble.

The psychotherapist will probably ask you to relax on a couch (though this is not a universal practice) while he helps you to understand more about your fears and their meaning.

Again, with this form of treatment it is necessary for you to face your fear. As you relax, you enter into the situation you fear, in imagination, and talk freely to the therapist about it, while he helps you to see the basic constituents in your anxieties. You will probably discuss the precipitating factor which triggered off your first terrible panic, and the background of events at that time.

Dreams

Your therapist will ask you to tell him your dreams, for if there are serious conflicts going on in the unconscious they will probably come to the surface in a disguised form in your dreams. Elements of ego-weakness and insecurity will likewise be revealed. From his expert knowledge and training the therapist can see through the disguise, and will help you to discover the emotional difficulties that are troubling you. You will find these have a bearing on your phobia.

Free Association

Apart from this, you will probably be asked to engage from time to time in what is known as 'free association' — which simply means that you allow your mind to wander (or free-wheel) and think aloud, sharing your thoughts and feelings with your therapist. Such thinking inevitably gravitates to the conflicts that are there below the surface. I say 'inevitably' — and that is true, as long as the association really is free and uninhibited.

The trouble is that pain, fear, embarrassment or guilt can act as a resistance against letting your thoughts and feelings go just where they will. Unconsciously you will tend to put the brake on them, or 'edit' them, and the therapist has to recognize what is happening and help you over the difficulty.

You will also meet with this factor of resistance when you try to recapture the painful experiences and feelings of childhood, where the root of your trouble lies. Again the therapist will make you aware of this resistance, and give you his reassurance and help so that you can overcome your fears. (There are, in fact, still further aspects of resistance, which I deal with in Chapter Ten.)

The Original Anxiety

As the analytic work proceeds, you will discover the reason why your panic is so exaggerated: it does not belong to your present-day experience at all. It is being 'projected' on to these situations, but really it refers to anxiety felt in your earliest years.

In the course of your therapy you will be encouraged to go back into those feelings, in imagination. This is not the same sort of imaginative work as that used in desensitization, for here you are going back in fantasy to the original experience, which aroused such panic that you probably thought you were being annihilated.

In the early situation it was a matter of life and death, or so it felt to you at the time. Tiny infants cannot see beyond their anxiety. They cannot look ahead and know that the danger will pass. The present moment is eternity. They have no means of knowing that their fears are exaggerated. They can use no powers of reason to help themselves.

The whole life of an infant in its early months consists of feeling. Security is life; anxiety is death. No wonder your panic is so great, when it relates, in fact, to the time when you actually thought this was the end.

It is also true that an infant's emotions, when experienced very strongly, are felt to be dangerous *in themselves*. It is as though the baby fears being overwhelmed and destroyed by the very force of emotions which he cannot control. This is another source of the very real panic felt by agoraphobics.

Such early emotions and anxieties can be brought back to consciousness with the help of a trained therapist. This is the analytic part of the therapy. What of the cure? Does the trouble disappear when you discover its true cause?

It is possible, of course, that the agoraphobia will be much relieved, or disappear altogether, when the patient sees that it is a spurious fear: when the true significance of the fear is brought to light and seen for what it is. It may well take some further work, however, before the trouble is cured.

Therapy

It is obvious that what has to be done now is to deal with the *true* anxiety which has been brought to the surface. For instance, if the anxiety is connected with guilt, then the guilt complex has to be dealt with. If it comes from a fear of isolation, then the therapy is directed towards this.

You may wonder how a therapist can free you from your complexes, inhibitions and conflicts. How does the *therapy* work? It is difficult to give a straightforward, simple answer to this question, in view of the many differing needs of patients, each of whom has his own particular background, his own individual problems, and his own response to different forms of therapy. It is also true that therapists work in different ways.

In general it may be said that two features are common. Firstly, the therapist offers a consistent, supportive and accepting relationship to the patient, in the face of whatever the patient has to tell him. Whatever aggression, or guilt, immature dependence or other traits of character come to the surface, the therapist accepts the patient as he is, giving him a reassurance that he is safe and secure.

The importance of this relationship cannot be over-emphasized. Remember that the fear goes back to babyhood, and in the life of a tiny, dependent baby, relationship is paramount. It is the one source of security — *or* of insecurity and anxiety.

Secondly, the trained psychotherapist can also explain, or interpret, the patient's feelings and demonstrate how they came to be experienced, and why they caused such intense anxiety. This makes it possible for the patient to replace the negative emotions with the positive motivations which make for wholeness.

For example, if a woman suffering from agoraphobia is found, during analysis, to be the victim of sexual inhibitions, the therapist can, as the trouble comes to light, explain the deep roots of her inhibitions, and so help her to a positive and healthy view of intimacy and romance. He thus helps to free her *not only* from her agoraphobia, *but also* from the inhibitions which have greatly impoverished her life. She is enabled to go about more freely but, more than that, she can find fulfilment in richer, more satisfying relationships, because of settled conflicts.

You can see what psychotherapy aims to do. It not only makes you face up to your present fear, but it encourages you to see the deeper meaning behind it, so that emotional conflicts and weaknesses of long-standing are brought into the light of day and dealt with. This goes to the heart of the trouble, to the point from which any radical cure must begin.

Self Help

Earlier in this book I said that one feature of the anxiety experienced in agoraphobia is bewilderment. The patient keeps on asking: 'Why am I like this?' The same goes for the other members of the family. A husband says of his wife: 'It's so unlike her. She used to be full of spirits and ready to go out and enjoy herself, but suddenly she has lost her gaiety and become lethargic and fearful. It's completely mystifying. It doesn't make sense.'

Well, we have seen that it *does* make sense, if only you can discover the background to it all. But analytic psycho-therapists are not to be found easily in some parts of the world, and in any case such treatment is expensive. If you really want to get down to the grass roots let me suggest how you may help yourself to gain deeper insight into your own particular problem.

Tracing the Trouble to Its Source

1. Keep a private notebook for this purpose, and first write down the situations which make you fearful, noting especially what they have in common, and the exact feelings you experience.

2. Write down in detail, as clearly as you can remember it, the precipitating cause of your fear – that is, the incident which triggered it off. Do this as soon as you can, because some of the details can easily be lost sight of over a period of time, or remembered inaccurately.

3. Make a careful note, too, of the background of events prior to the incident, which may prove significant (as in the case I describe below). Include in this, particularly, anything which may have disturbed your equanimity in any way at all – a disagreement, disappointment, a criticism or injustice, embarrassment or conflict.

4. If your phobia was not triggered off suddenly, but came after a period of illness or difficulty of some sort, write down as much as you can recollect of your feelings at that time. Was there any sense of failure, or guilt, of inferiority or injustice, for example?

5. Practise the art of relaxation, as I described it in Chapter Seven. It is only when you are as relaxed as possible, physically and mentally, that you can allow your *feelings* to come to the surface.

6. Now you are ready to do some 'association'. Take yourself, in imagination, to some situation which fills you with terror – say, going into the shopping centre. Let your feelings have full rein, and see where they take you in memory or imagination. Where and when have you felt like this before? (By this I mean *prior* to the onset of your phobia, more probably in childhood or early infancy.)

7. What is the basic element in your fear? Are you, for instance, afraid of authority, or of the intensity of your emotions, or of being lost and forgotten? Are you afraid of being rejected and not wanted? Try to pin down the feeling if you can, and follow it as far as

possible to its most devastating conclusion, the ultimate in terror. Perhaps you feared utter rejection, or annihilation.

8. 'Associate' in this same way, with regard to the precipitating cause and its background as you have noted them (2. and 3.), or the emotional state you were in when you became phobic (4.). Where does this take you, if you let your feelings carry you back? Remember, it is the *feeling* which has association in the past, so concentrate on this as much as possible.

9. As you do this, you will probably begin to trace some history of your feelings back towards the original trauma which has *really* caused the trouble. It is unlikely that you will get to this in the course of just two or three attempts, but if you persevere, when you are able to get some time to relax, I am sure you will find some insights coming to you.

An Illustration

Let me give you an example which will illustrate some of the points I have mentioned. They concern the case of the army major, related by Dr Hadfield, to which I referred in Chapter Three.

You may remember his agoraphobia was precipitated one evening as he was crossing the camp to the officers' mess, in the Egyptian desert. He felt an awful dread of the darkness, the space and the solitariness. Associating to this, he recollected an episode at the age of six when he ran away from home one night, and found himself in an open field, filled with terror in the darkness. His self-will in running away had taken him into danger, and he returned home much chastened and became obedient and docile.

Some relief of his phobia followed when this memory came back, but his trouble was not cured. His associations took him further back, to an incident when, after a bout of naughtiness on his part, his rather cruel nurse took him by the throat and he felt his life to be in danger. It happened on the open sea-front, where no help was in sight, and he had no alternative but to submit. Again, in this earlier incident, his self-assertion had run him into danger.

The open space of the desert, the darkness and the solitariness had obvious associations with the past, but this was still not the final answer. Why did the major have a fit of panic on that *particular* evening? He had, after all, crossed the camp in the same way, and at the same time, night after night.

Further inquiry revealed that prior to the incident on the night in question, there had been an argument with a fellow officer. The major knew he was in the right and wanted to assert himself, yet he feared the row involved. There was a further complication, in that if he gave in and did as the other officer wanted, he would find himself faced with a court martial for breaking regulations! It was this conflict (should he assert himself or should he give in?) which really lay behind the phobia, and this insight brought him release.

You can see, here again, the difference between the two types of therapy I have described. The major might have been freed from his agoraphobia by some form of desensitization treatment. But the more radical approach of psychotherapy revealed the *real* trouble. With the therapists's help he was enabled to acquire a new confidence in his own personality, and in his right to assert himself when necessary. His life-long conflict concerning authority, which had been repressed in the unconscious, was resolved.

Re-educating Your Emotions

The latter point brings me to the fact that when you have gained insight into the cause of your problem you must set about re-educating your emotions. Almost certainly you will have discovered that some form of early insecurity lies behind your trouble. Recognize that this was all in the past. Because of your helplessness you were devastated by it at the time. It was felt as a threat to your very survival. But that is over now. You can put it behind you. Your existence is no longer threatened.

Nurture yourself in feelings of inner security. Affirm the validity of your own personality – it is your birthright. You will find that when you become more secure as a person life begins to open up. As you become motivated by positive aims, instead of the need to cope with inner conflicts, inhibitions and anxiety, it will make a *tremendous* difference to your life.

CHAPTER TEN

RESISTANCE

It may seem very strange to you when I say that your efforts to break free from your prison of agoraphobia will inevitably meet with resistance. No, not from the family: they will be only too pleased to have you restored to your usual active self! Oddly enough it is *you* who will resist getting better. It is very important that you should recognize this and understand it, because if you are aware of the danger you will be on your guard against it.

It is true to say that every person who suffers from an emotional disorder tends, *unconsciously*, to sabotage his own attempts to put things right. Let me explain this more fully.

One part of you — your rational, intelligent self — is quite determined to find a way through your dilemma, and to enjoy life normally and fully once more. But you must remember that your phobia serves a very real purpose in the unconscious.

Defence

We have seen that your phobia is a *defence against a still deeper fear* — a basic insecurity in one form or another. This insecurity dates from a time when you were *utterly helpless* and quite unable to cope with your terror. It seemed a threat to your very survival. You could not counter it by argument, nor could you look ahead to the time when it would pass. You did the only possible thing, if you were to survive. You repressed the fear, and the cause of it, deeply in your unconscious. The intensity of that panic reasserts itself on occasion today, but you no longer feel *totally* insecure — you have projected the original fear on to the fear of the street, so that you can now deal with it: you can avoid the panic by staying indoors. So this new fear is a *defence – against feeling the even more terrifying fear* you experienced as a child. Such a defence is not going to be given up lightly.

False Security
Unconsciously you even find a certain security in your present position. You have been imprisoned by your fear for a long time. The prison is uninteresting and monotonous and has severe disadvantages perhaps. You long to be free. But the prison also has one advantage: it has a certainty about it. You know where you are in this prison. This is the way of life to which you have adapted yourself – it is familiar ground.

By contrast, the world of freedom offers you adventure, new experiences and new friends. Can you take all this? Can you bear to leave the prison, with its certainty (unsatisfactory though it is) to find your freedom? (You may remember the dream of Dr Guntrip's patient, which I quoted in Chapter Five; it also has relevance here.)

I want you to understand that I am not merely talking here in terms of the *house* being your prison where you feel safe – it is something much more fundamental and more subtle than that. I am referring to your emotional 'life-style'. Its very uniformity gives you a 'safe' feeling. (To illustrate this point from other disorders, I could say that the invalid may feel more at home with illness than with good health; the victim of depression is in familiar territory when he is in the throes of despair; the 'martyr' finds satisfaction in his martyrdom – and so on.) The 'safety' is not well-founded, but it feels better than nothing.

Compensations
It is possible that you are finding other compensations, too, from your present situation. It is a fact of human nature that we do find consolation in our distresses, and a good thing we do: it helps us to overcome our disappointments.

A man who loses the chance of a better job with another firm may be comforted by the knowledge that he would have had to move to a district where the housing position could be very difficult. Or you may lose a dress you saw in the shop window a short time ago, and you console yourself with the thought that at least you have saved your money!

We adapt ourselves to circumstances in this way, and on the whole it makes for a more positive, contented life. But when our health is at·stake (physically, mentally or emotionally) it is a very different matter. For we are in danger of accepting negative satisfactions (illness, anxiety, guilt, etc.) instead of the *real* wealth of happiness, health and fulfilment.

Your phobia may have brought you sympathy and attention, even significance (which is something every one of us needs). Perhaps your family or friends show a concern for you – more than they did before. It could also be that because of your 'disablement' you manage to escape other duties or responsibilities that you used to find irksome: social visits, looking after elderly in-laws, etc.

Unconscious Motivations

Let me say at once that in no way am I 'getting at you' or criticizing you. There is no condemnation implied or intended in anything I am saying here. You are the one who is suffering; you *want* consciously to be free. But it is important that you should be alive to the *unconscious motivations* which will drag you into accepting 'substitute' satisfactions instead of the real thing.

Dependence

Finally a word about another possible source of resistance: your own dependent needs. You may remember that one feature of most agoraphobes is their 'ego-weakness' – their need to cling to the safety of home. This has yet another facet.

Patients who are very dependent have great difficulty in regard to relationships with other people. They hunger for love, yet they fear to trust it when it comes. It *could* be that an agoraphobic wife is unconsciously trying to keep her partner at home, to reassure her of his love. If there has been any underlying doubt about the other's love, the agoraphobia may be a desperate attempt to divert attention to oneself.

Another result of this difficulty in making relationships is that the patient shies away from social activities and retires into his shell, his own inner world. It is not a satisfactory world, and it has its own anxiety, but again it has some feeling of certainty and safety about it.

It may take a long time for you to become fully aware of this factor of resistance. Indeed you will resist becoming aware of it. (I suspect you are already rebelling, as you read this.) There is such a desperate need to cling to the old way of life, the old emotional pattern, which is familiar. The forces of resistance are very deep-rooted and subtle.

But you cannot have it both ways. You must make the choice. You can have the old negative, restricted life you have been living in recent years, or be prepared to accept new, positive goals of happiness and fulfilment. You can stay in the dark tunnel of your fear and frustration. But there is light at the end of the tunnel and *you can decide* to follow that light into the open, to a life of freedom and greater joy than you have known for many a year. Do I hear you saying: 'I haven't the courage'? That is the voice of resistance, of your unconscious saboteur! Be *wholly determined* to go forward, and then you will find the courage to take the first step.

CHAPTER ELEVEN

WHAT ABOUT MY CHILDREN?

Many agoraphobic mothers are concerned, and rightly so, about the effects of their own trouble on their children. I understand that members of 'The Open Door' have recently taken part in a project to find out how agoraphobia develops in children. The organization has also collated information about the incidence of agoraphobia within families.

The Question of Heredity

In his book *Fears and Phobias*, Dr Isaac Marks[1] has said: 'There is no firm evidence that genetic inheritance plays a significant part in the development of phobic states in particular patients.' He goes on to report that in a survey of phobic patients 19 per cent of agoraphobics reported that they had a close relative with the same kind of phobia: not a large percentage.

I think there is little doubt that the child's early environment is a more important factor than heredity as such. A child is so easily influenced by the attitudes of his mother, and if she is nervous and frightened out of doors (or in), the child will probably acquire the same feelings.

I am not a child psychiatrist, however; nor is my concern limited to the possibility of your child becoming agoraphobic. As a practising psychotherapist, I am thinking about his, or her, general emotional stability. For the children of today may become the patients of tomorrow, if their early environment is not helpful.

[1] Dr Isaac Marks: *Fears and Phobias*, Heinemann Medical Books.

Practical Issues

Leaving aside the question of genetic factors, the importance of which is not yet established, how far is it likely that a mother's phobia will affect her children? I think the answer depends on many different factors.

Some mothers can accompany their families on at least some outings. For others who cannot leave the house at all, the position is much more difficult. In the latter case, it will be helpful if there are older children who are willing and able to take the younger ones out. If their father is good with the children, and is able to go out with them and join in their fun, it will be easier for them than if he is tied up with business affairs for long hours, or if he finds it difficult to identify himself with their needs.

If the mother is widowed, or separated from her husband, so that she has the sole care of the children, the problem will be greater still.

The family may live in a house with a garden, where the children can get plenty of fresh air and sunshine; this is obviously better for both their health and their spirits than if they are cooped up in a sky-scraper block of flats, with few facilities near at hand.

If there are grandparents or other relatives living close by, so that the youngsters can visit them on occasions, or if such relatives can have them for holidays, this will be a boon.

The Vital Factor

I do want to emphasize, however, that it is not the practical issues which are the most important, by any means. The lack of outings and holidays is something that a child will get over. But earlier in this book I discussed one factor which is vital in any child's emotional development – *relationship*. You may find this some consolation if you have been feeling guilty about your children missing some treats which others get.

It must also be a challenge – especially if you are one of those unfortunate victims caught up in a general anxiety state, and have become withdrawn and unable to rouse yourself to take much interest in other people's affairs. You *must* be genuinely interested in your children's lives if you are to be a real mother to them.

Remember, too, that little things mean a lot to children. Matters which seem trivial to you will loom large in their lives. It is important for you to bear this in mind, for you may be so devastated by your own problems that you feel other people's troubles are as nothing compared with yours. This will not be helpful where a child is involved.

Security

One of the deepest needs which your relationship should meet is that of security. You may have difficulties here. If you are holding your baby in your arms while you are petrified with fear yourself, or even feeling nervy and edgy, your child will sense your fear, and react in the same way. He will feel insecure.

Another facet of this problem arises where the atmosphere in the home has become strained, for no child feels secure if the relationship on which the home has been founded is uncertain.

Most children run to mother for safety if they are frightened; yours will look to *you* to be their tower of strength. This will demand a lot from you, but if you can concentrate on giving your little ones the love and security they need, you may well find your own troubles receding. Your concern for them will help to take your mind off your own fears.

Above all it is the security of your *love* which they need. A warm, tender, yet non-possessive relationship is the most precious thing you can offer them in the first few years of their life. They can survive a lot of disadvantages if they have this one 'pearl of great price'. In this lies your vocation as a mother, and in fulfilling it you will find that your own life is greatly enriched.

Some General Advice

If you already have children, let them go out as much as

possible; encourage them to be independent. Conceal your own fears from them if you possibly can, or they will tend to adopt your own attitudes. Avoid *at all costs* the temptation to lean on them for company, no matter how hard this is for you.

Remember it is not always easy to assess what is going on in a child's emotions. If there are outward signs of distress or upset, like persistent bed-wetting, tantrums, stealing and so on, then you know something is wrong. Unfortunately the reverse is not so certain: a child may appear to be quite unaffected by factors in his early environment, but then in adolescence or later life he can be overcome by feelings of inadequacy, fears, or other emotional disorders which are traced to infant insecurity.

Perhaps you are considering the advisability or otherwise of having a child, and wondering whether or not this would help you to overcome your phobia.

There are patients who have *become* agoraphobic after childbirth; there are others whose phobic troubles have greatly improved after the birth of another child.

One thing is important: do not have a child *for the purpose* of helping you out of your troubles. This would be wrong. One sometimes hears it said: 'I think a baby would help us to hold our marriage together' or 'I think it's a good idea to have a child in later life: it helps to keep you young.' Do not adopt this kind of attitude in regard to your own problems. It is quite wrong to have a child with the unconscious expectation that the baby will do anything at all *for you*. One cannot and must not put any 'responsibility' on to a baby. If things do not turn out as you had hoped (if, in your case, your agoraphobia persists) you will be resentful. You may find the child a burden, without the advantage you hoped to get in compensation.

If you think of having children, do so only because of the joy you will know in expressing your love in this way, and the delight of seeing them grow up happy and independent. Your motive must be, in other words, an 'out-going' one.

Lastly, do not limit your thinking to the problem of

whether your children will be affected by your phobia. Look forward, instead, to your emancipation. Your children cannot cure your phobia, but they can give you the necessary incentive so that *for their sakes* and your own, you explore every avenue open to you in a determined effort to find release.

CHAPTER TWELVE

OVER TO YOU

There is one more thing I want to say to you, if you suffer from agoraphobia. It is this: you may be somewhat disappointed that this book has offered no easy solution, no ready answer which can put you out of your misery right away.

You may have been hoping that I could have done just that. You secretly look for a 'magic formula' which will eradicate your panic and fear in a flash. It is a very natural wish.

Your Responsibility

I remember how, in my previous work as a college lecturer, a student would sometimes ask me (almost aggressively) at the outset of the course, just what percentage of my students passed their examination in the previous year. He was, of course, putting the onus solely on *me* to get him through his course successfully. Such a student always came to learn that though I was willing to do everything I possibly could to help him, ultimately it was his own responsibility. I could not, for example, inject knowledge into his head, nor the ability to express himself succinctly and accurately. I was there to help him and guide him in his study, but it was his own work and determination which would get him through.

It is the same with emotional problems. Unfortunately it is not possible to obtain an injection of 'instant courage'. Nor is it possible to get rid of panic like one gets rid of an aching tooth — in one short, sharp operation.

A surgeon can remove a troublesome appendix without a great deal of help from you — all he needs is your signature on the consent form for the anaesthetic. If psychotherapy could be administered in the same way, how much easier it would be! But here the personality is involved – and that means your own will, your own brave, honest attempt to face up to your problems and weaknesses.

However many books you read, however many people you contact for advice, if you are putting the responsibility for a 'cure' on to someone else you will be disappointed, and possibly bitter.

'Nobody Understands'

One of the complaints of agoraphobics, as I have mentioned before, is that 'nobody understands'. This is one grievance to which you may turn time and time again, when really what you are doing is evading the issue. If some suggestion made to you is uncongenial, if the task seems too heavy, the challenge too great, you may well be tempted to shelter behind that well-worn phrase 'You don't understand'. You can go on like this for ever.

Indeed the lack of understanding can actually become 'libidinized' – by which I mean that you can actually live on your martyrdom; you can make a meal of it.

You may even be seething with indignation as you are reading this chapter. At least, you hoped, here would be one person who would know how helpless you are to help yourself. I know how you feel. I do understand how hard it is for you to believe that there is, in fact, anything you can do to help yourself. How easy it is for someone else to tell you what to do!

The First Move

I do wish I had an easier solution to offer to you. But there is none that I know of. You will have to accept the fact that if you are looking to someone else to help you out of your slough of despond without any real initiative on your part, then you are asking the impossible. It is like trying to lift someone who is physically unable to help himself. When the patient is a dead weight there is so little you can do, and if he can give no co-operation, when you cease to support him he falls back where he was before. This is no good – and you know it in your heart.

Courage is required to accept the fact that *you and you alone* can ultimately *ensure* your cure. If you have not the courage to face *that* fact, then you must accept the fact that you will spend the rest of your days in your old familiar prison.

If you do seek help from any source – your doctor, a therapist, 'The Open Door' organization, or a writer who sets out to help you with your problem, you must expect to *play your part*. It has to be a joint effort. *You* must play the game, and the ball is in *your* court. The first move is yours.

At the end of the day, however, there is a prize to be won – and what a worth-while one it is! I cannot give you 'instant courage', but I can give you my understanding, and my encouragement to take the first step.

In Chapter Eight I told you of Mrs A., the widow who, after eleven years of being confined to the house, made a brave attempt to visit a former foster-child, and came back alone by bus. Her article ended with these words: 'The only thing that maddens me is that I did not try years ago'. Will that be *your* regret in several years' time? I sincerely hope not.

Conclusion

Agoraphobia is distressing, debilitating and depressing. You long for freedom, fulfilment and fun. Is it really possible to achieve the transformation? Can agoraphobia *really* be cured? The answer to that is most definitely 'yes' – if you really want to do it.

I have not suggested that the path is easy. It will take time to change the emotional habits of several years. But it can be done.

You, as the sufferer, know to what extent your own problem restricts and embarrasses you. You alone know what you expect from a cure. If your sole aim is to be free to go out, to go on holidays, etc., then some course of desensitization should help you enormously. Your own doctor will no doubt be able to tell you the nearest hospital where you can obtain such treatment, or there may be a psychotherapist in your area who can help you. If it is quite impossible for you to get to a trained therapist, then you can do a lot to help yourself, as I have suggested in Chapters Seven and Eight. There are scores of people who can vouch for the release that this type of therapy affords. It has helped others, and it can help you, if you have the same determination.

But you must make the first move. No one ever crossed the ocean without leaving the shore; and no one ever crossed the threshold without opening the door. That first, positive step is so very important.

Remember that the weakness you feel is not so much physical as emotional. By that I mean that it is your emotional state which is producing the physical symptoms. But remember, too, that the longer you stay put in your home, refusing to leave the house, the weaker your legs are going to feel. If you have not been getting normal exercise your muscles will probably have become a little flabby.

Of course you feel strange at first. You may know from experience that a patient who comes home after a long stay in hospital feels quite odd at first in the outside world. Indeed, I remember that after a six months' stay in hospital I myself felt *terribly* strange, even in the living room of my own home. Can you wonder that after being in the house for so long — years perhaps — you feel strange and somewhat at a loss when you venture into the street?

Do not be misled into thinking this feeling is some sort of illness or terrible cause for alarm. It will take time for you to re-orientate yourself in the world of cars and buses, or crowded supermarkets and open parks, from which you have withdrawn yourself for so long.

Every day you put if off, the more difficult it will become for you to make that first effort. But your recovery lies, not in thinking and wondering and wishing, but in *doing* — in taking that first positive step.

Some of you who read this book will recognize that

merely to go out freely again is not the answer to the deepest needs of your own personality. You know that there are other factors which are robbing you of your true potential. You will only be satisfied if you can get to the *source* of the trouble and put that right.

Treating a sick plant is all very well. But if something is eating at the root, or if it is growing in the wrong soil, the plant will be weak, however much it is treated on the surface. Likewise if jealousy, frustration, bitterness or guilt is eating at the root of your emotional life, then your personality is being impaired. Or if, unfortunately, the environment in which you spent your earliest years failed to provide the right conditions for healthy, stable emotional development, then the 'soil' needs changing. You need to make a fresh start, to grow up again emotionally, in an atmosphere of security and self-acceptance, so that you acquire a positive and fulfilling philosophy of life.

Analytic therapy, where it is available, can provide the answer for those who prefer this more radical approach to their problem. But psychotherapy, too, can be painful. To live again through one's fears and insecurity, in order to understand them and find freedom from them, does take courage. But only those who have gone that way, and found complete release from their problem know what it means to become a new person. The cathartic nature of such an experience cannot be denied. It makes for wholeness and maturity of personality.

To be, or not to be, that is the question! The choice is yours. Only you can make the decision. No one can force you to do anything you do not wish to do, and without your own determination and co-operation *any* therapist is helpless.

You can remain in your prison, with your fears, and with all the worry and distress and frustration which is entailed for you and your family. Or you can go forward, knowing that *there is a way through your fear, to freedom and to fulfilment.*